Guillaume, Alfred, 1888-
The influence of Judaism

Bevan, Edwyn Robert, 1870- *ed.* The legacy of Israel ... 1927. (Card 2)

CONTENTS—Continued.

influence of Judaism on Islam, by the Rev. A. Guillaume.—The Jewish factor in medieval thought, by C. Singer and Dorothea W. Singer.—Hebrew scholarship in the middle ages among Latin Christians, by C. Singer.—Hebrew studies in the reformation period and after: their place and influence, by the Rev. G. H. Box.—The influence of Judaism on western law, by N. Isaacs.—The influence of the Old Testament on Puritanism, by the Rev. W. B. Selbie.—Jewish thought in the modern world, by L. Roth.—Influence of the Hebrew Bible on European languages, by A. Meillet.—The legacy in modern literature, by L. Magnus.—Epilogue, by C. G. Montefiore.—Glossary.

1. Jews—Civilization. 2. Jews—Hist. I. Singer, Charles Joseph, 1876- joint ed. II. Title.

Library of Congress DS113.B45 27-27955

[3-3]

THE
Traditions of
ISLAM

THE

Traditions of ISLAM

An Introduction to the study of the HADITH LITERATURE

By Alfred Guillaume, M.A.

Professor of Hebrew and Oriental Languages in the University of Durham.

Sometime Hody Exhibitioner of Wadham College, Oxford.

OXFORD

AT THE CLARENDON PRESS

1924

Oxford University Press
London Edinburgh Glasgow Copenhagen
New York Toronto Melbourne Cape Town
Bombay Calcutta Madras Shanghai
Humphrey Milford Publisher to the UNIVERSITY

Printed in England

PREFACE

It is a curious fact that an empire containing more than a hundred million Muslims has not produced a book in the English language dealing with and explaining a great branch of Muhammadan literature which stands beside the Quran as a source of Muslim belief and practice. The lack of such a book on the traditions of Islam is difficult to explain, because the everyday life of Muslims throughout the world is governed and directed by these traditions. But, at any rate, it absolves the author from the necessity for an apology for venturing to treat of so vast a subject.

I need not point out my indebtedness to the work of older scholars, particularly the late Ignaz Goldziher, whose *Muhammedanische Studien* must form the basis of any work on the *ḥadīth* literature. Scholars will recognize that I have drawn freely from his writings, and this acknowledgement of my indebtedness must suffice. I have not, however, shirked the obvious duty of studying the literature at first hand, especially in the *Kanzu-l-'Ummāl*, compiled by 'Alā-al-Dīn b. Muttaqī of Burhanpur, who died in 975 A.H., and in the *Mishkātu-l-Maṣābīḥ*, 'The Niche of the Lamps,' an anthology of tradition selected by Wālīu-l-Dīn Abū 'Abd Allah (*fl.* 737), and based on the *Maṣābīḥu-l-Sunna* of Muhammad Abū Muhammad Al Baghawī (d. 516). It would be difficult to over-estimate the value of the *Mishkāt* as a synopsis of the ḥadīth literature. The author has (*a*) omitted the *isnād* or chain of narrators of each tradition, (*b*) arranged his material according to the subject-matter with sub-divisions of 'genuine', 'good', and 'weak' authority, (*c*) ranged almost the whole field of the literature, and (*d*) given a representative selection of the traditions free from the constant repetitions occurring in almost all the original collections. I have not always been careful to cite the individual author from whom the anthologist has culled his hadith, because a most laborious search would be necessary to determine whether a parallel hadith was preserved by other writers, and the point is often of no importance. Moreover, when the great concordance to hadith, which is now being prepared by Professor Wensinck, of Leyden, with the assistance of many British and Continental Arabists, has been published the curious will be able at a glance to determine such questions for themselves. Nor do I propose to notice the prolific growth of compendia and commentaries to hadith which form excrescences on the original literature.

The Shīʿa collections of traditions deserve a separate treatise, and are not dealt with in these pages.

I cannot hope in a work of this size to have given more than an outline of a vast territory which has not yet been opened up to the Western student.

Experience as a political officer in the Arab Bureau during the war convinced me of the importance of hadith. I have, for instance, seen it invoked by doctors to settle the question as to whether the faithful might eat horseflesh, and by Bolshevists to persuade Muhammadans that republics are of divine appointment.

My thanks are due to my friend Sir Thomas Arnold, who first suggested this undertaking to me, and who has constantly assisted me with helpful criticism; and to Professor Margoliouth, without whose advice no old pupil of his would venture to write on matters Arabian. Finally, I desire to express my deep gratitude to the Librarians and sub-Librarians of the India Office and the Indian Institute, Oxford, who lent me for long periods books which were otherwise inaccessible.

CONTENTS

3

I

THE EVOLUTION OF HADITH

Meaning and use of the word hadith *and its relation to* sunna.—*Are any* hadith *genuine?—Their genesis and historical value.—When were* hadith *first written down?—Authorities contradict one another.—Mālik's Muwaṭṭa.—Musnad of Aḥmad.—The six canonical collections, Bukhārī, Muslim, Abu Dāūd, Al Tirmidhī, Ibn Māja, and Al Nasāī.—Other collections.*

INQUIRY into the content, scope, and character of the traditions of Islam must necessarily begin after the death of Muhammad; for the *raison d'être* of this vast literature is to provide an authoritative standard of belief and conduct based upon the word and deed of Muhammad which shall be binding upon the whole of the Muhammadan world. It is notorious that though the Quran contains a certain number of laws, e.g. rules in regard to marriage, inheritances, and the care of orphans, it cannot be successfully invoked to settle questions arising in such diverse categories as systematic and moral theology, ritual, and civil and military law. The Jews found the Mosaic law with its wealth of detail insufficient by itself without the assistance of case law and tradition, and the Talmud arose to supply this need. Similarly, the Muhammadan community found itself at the death of Muhammad with a holy book and the living memory of a prophet; from these two sources the ecclesiastical and temporal polity of the Islamic world was for all time built up.

The word *ḥadīth* is a noun formed from the verb *ḥadatha* 'to be new' (cf. the Hebrew *ḥadash* with the same meaning and the noun *ḥodesh* 'new moon'). Properly hadith means 'news' and then a tale or verbal communication of any kind. It may with propriety be used of an account of a tribal raid, of old sagas, of incidents in the life of the prophet, and even of the Quran itself. The great impetus given to religious thought and speculation by Muhammad and the Quran could not fail to influence the language of Muhammadan writers, and thus the word has acquired its narrowed technical connotation of an oral tradition which can be traced back to a Companion or to the prophet Muhammad. Arabic preserves clearly the consciousness of the special connotation given to the word *hadith*, for Bukhārī records a saying of 'Abd Allah b. Mas'ūd that 'the best hadith is the book of God',[1] and of the prophet in reply to Abū Huraira's question, 'Who will be the happiest on the day of resurrection thanks to your intercession?' 'I thought you would be the first to inquire of me about this hadith because I have noticed your eagerness in regard to the hadith.'[2]

Hadith enshrines the *sunna* or 'beaten track'—the custom and practice of the old Muhammadan community. Inasmuch as hadith were often invoked to prove that a certain act was performed by the prophet, and was therefore to be imitated by all pious believers, it follows that hadith and sunna are sometimes names for one and the same thing. But there is no necessary connexion between them, and we often find that tradition is in conflict with custom. The great merit

[1] Bāb I'tiṣām, ed. Krehl, iv, p. 420.

[2] Bāb Riqāq 51, Krehl, iv, p. 245.

of Mālik b. Anas in the eyes of his contemporaries was that he was an authority both on custom law and on oral tradition. Perhaps the best example of the distinction is in the title of a book cited by the Fihrist, 'the book of the sunnas with confirmatory hadith'.[1]

The conservatism of the East has long been proverbial, and the Arab may fairly claim a share in the building up of this reputation. The acceptance of monotheism, it is true, marked a break with the past; but the prophet was careful to depart as little as possible from the path of his forefathers. Indeed, it may be said that in the Medina *suras* he appears as the restorer of the ancient faith of Arabia—the religion of Ibrāhīm Abū Isma'īl.[2] The word *sunna* up to the time of Muhammad meant the practice of antiquity: after his time it acquired in orthodox circles a different significance, and came to denote the practice of the prophet and his immediate successors. The same hatred of innovation finds expression in the utterances of the savants of Medina as in those of their heathen forefathers. Medina naturally became the 'home of the sunna', because there lived the men who had first to adapt their lives to the teaching of the prophet; thus, so far as corporate life was concerned, Medina was the authority on questions of orthodox custom.

The reverence in which the prophet was held by his contemporaries, and more especially by those who had

[1] p. 230, 3. The word *hadith* throughout this book will be used both as a singular and a collective noun. *Hadiths* is scarcely possible in English, and the constant employment of the Arabic broken plural *aḥādīth* is hardly to be desired.

[2] See the illuminating observations of Père H. Lammens in *Une adaptation arabe du monothéisme biblique*.

never seen him in the flesh, naturally led them to preserve and repeat his sayings on all subjects. The feverish desire to know what he had said and done, which is well marked in the second generation, increased in intensity until it reached its height in the absurdities of the exercise known as *Ṭalabu-l-'Ilm.*[1] The foundation of the enormous mass of traditions which afterwards accumulated was laid by the Companions who were scattered throughout the Muhammadan world; but it would be rash to dogmatize as to how much of existing material can be safely ascribed to them. Our estimate of traditions circulated in their name cannot but be adversely affected by the frequent accusations of forgery levelled against many of the professional traditionists, by the many anachronisms they contain, and by the political and sectarian bias they display.[2] When all these factors are allowed for, and account is taken of the inevitable mistakes that must occur when traditions are handed down through a long line of speakers, it is difficult to regard the hadith literature as a whole as an accurate and trustworthy record of the sayings and doings of Muhammad. But however sceptical we are with regard to the ultimate historical value of the traditions, it is hard to overrate their importance in the formation of the life of the Islamic races throughout the centuries. If we cannot accept them at their face value, they are of inestimable value as a mirror of the events which preceded the

[1] *Infra*, p. 36.

[2] 'The number of motives leading to the fabrication of traditions was so great that the historian is in constant danger of employing as veracious records what were deliberate fictions.'—Margoliouth, *Mohammed and the Rise of Islam*, London, 1905, p. vi.

consolidation of Islam into a system. Many of the political, dynastic, religious, and social differences which agitated Islam in the days of its imperial might are illustrated in traditions promulgated by the conflicting parties in the interest of their pretensions. In them we see how the rival forces of militarism and pacificism, asceticism and materialism, mysticism and literalism, free will and determinism, strove fiercely for the mastery.

While the prophet was alive he was the sole guide in all matters whether spiritual or secular. Hadith, or tradition in the technical sense, may be said to have begun at his death, for the extraordinary influence of his personality on his companions and associates created from the beginning a demand that believers should be informed what the prophet had done and taught in various circumstances in order that the life of the community and the individual might be modelled on that of the revered leader. But of the resultant mass of tradition few can be confidently regarded as emanating from the authorities whose names they bear. The veneration of a later generation for the prophet is well illustrated in a hadith quoted by Muir: 'Is it possible, father of ʿAbd Allah, that thou hast been with Muhammad?' was the question addressed by a pious Muslim to Ḥudhaifa, in the mosque of Al Kūfa; 'Didst thou really see the prophet, and wert thou on terms of familiar intercourse with him?' 'Son of my uncle! it is indeed as thou sayest.' 'And how wert thou wont to behave towards the prophet?' 'Verily we used to labour hard to please him.' 'Well, by the Lord!' exclaimed the ardent listener, 'if I had been but alive in his time, I would not have allowed him to put his blessed foot upon the earth, but would have borne him on my shoulders wheresoever he listed.'[1]

During the reign of the first four caliphs the energies of the Arabs were mainly directed to the expansion of their empire. The amazing rapidity of their conquests left little time, even if the inclination were present, to preach and teach the faith. A people which within a century had made itself master of the races and lands lying between the Atlantic and the Oxus could not be extensively preoccupied in religious matters. Nor must it be supposed that there was a fixed and established cultus and theory of an ordered religious life even in the prophet's own town. Possibly in Medina, where, under the personal influence of Muhammad, men devoted themselves to the things of religion, an ecclesiastical usage may have developed quite early in the first century; in the provinces where Arabs represented but a mere fraction of proselytized nations no such usage existed. With the army went Companions and Followers, who must have carried with them some traditional religious customs; but in the earliest days Medina itself had no fixed system of jurisprudence, indeed it was then hardly developing. The natural result was a wide divergence in practice between many of the provinces of the empire, which has continued down to the present day in the Muslim world. Echoes of this state of affairs can sometimes be heard in the hadith literature: Abu Dāūd constantly calls attention to the purely local character of some hadith (*infarada ahl* of such and such a place).

[1] *Life of Muhammad*, revised by T. H. Weir, Edinburgh, 1912, p. xxx. (In this edition the references to the original sources are omitted.)

The hadith literature as we now have it provides us with apostolic precept and example covering the whole duty of man: it is the basis of that developed system of law, theology, and custom which is Islam. Now inasmuch as the bulk of this literature is demonstrably the work of the two hundred and fifty years after the prophet's death, it is necessary, in endeavouring to determine the age and early authority of hadith, to examine the very considerable amount of evidence for the existence of hadith written down during the life of the prophet. This evidence has been collected by Sprenger[1], who also quotes what claims to be early evidence to the contrary. Of the series authorizing the writing of hadith we may cite one on the authority of that prolific father of tradition Abū Huraira, who says that one of the Helpers (Anṣār) used to sit and listen with admiration to the utterances of the prophet of God, and, being unable to remember what he heard, lamented his weakness to the prophet. The latter replied, 'Call your right hand to your aid,' i.e. write them down. This hadith exists in many different forms associated with the names of Abu Ṣāliḥ and Anas b. Mālik. Again, 'Abd Allah b. 'Umar says: 'We said, "O prophet of God, we hear from you hadith which we cannot remember. May we not write them down?" "By all means write them down," said he.' This hadith exists in no less than thirty versions, which present small differences. Again, Abū Huraira asserts—not without reason!—that none of the Companions preserved more hadith than he, except 'Abd

[1] *On the origin and progress of writing down historical facts among the Musulmans.* (*Journal of the Asiatic Society of Bengal*, 1856, pp. 303–29.)

Allah b. 'Umar. 'But he wrote them down, and I did not write them.' This 'Abd Allah (d. 65) says, 'The book I wrote from the prophet of God is Al Ṣadīqa,' and Mujāhid asserts that he saw this book in the possession of its compiler. Anas b. Mālik states that Abū Bakr wrote down for him the laws regarding alms. Abundant proof could be adduced that books were read and written by the early Arabs; it will suffice to quote a saying attributed to Dhu'l Rumma (d. 117), in which he expresses his dislike of those who rely on their memories instead of writing down poetry: 'Write down my poetry, for the written word is more pleasing to me than memory. . . . A book does not forget, nor does it substitute one word for another.'

Probably the hadith literature presents us with more contradictory statements on the question as to whether it was permissible to write down traditions of the prophet in the early days of Islam than on any other question. Many express prohibitions can be quoted. Abū Sa'īd al Khudrī asserts that he asked the prophet's permission to write down hadith, and it was refused. Abū Huraira is reported to have said: 'The prophet of God came out to us while we were writing hadith, and said, "What is this that you are writing?" We said, "Hadith which we hear from thee." Said he, "A book other than the book of God! Do you not know that nothing but the writing of books beside the book of God led astray the peoples that were before you?" We said, "Are we to relate hadith of you, O prophet of God?" He replied, "Relate hadith of me: there is no objection. But he who intentionally speaks falsely on my authority will find a place in hell."' In one version Abū Huraira adds that the writings were heaped together and burned. Further Abū Nadhra relates: 'We said to Abū Sa'īd: "Would that you would write down hadith for us, for we cannot remember them." He answered: "We will not write them, nor will we collect them in books. The prophet of God related them to us orally and we remembered them, so you must do the same."' The comment of Ibn 'Aun (d. 151) on the situation is not without interest. He says: 'The men of the first century who disapproved of writing held that principle in order that the Muslims might not be kept by other books from the study of the Quran. The ancient scriptures have been forbidden because it is impossible to distinguish what is true in them from what is false and the genuine from the spurious: moreover the Quran renders them superfluous.'

As a matter of fact, the controversy as to whether it was lawful or not to write down traditions really belongs to the age when the critical collections of traditions were made. The hadith last quoted do not invalidate the statements that traditions were written down from the mouth of the prophet; the extraordinary importance attached to every utterance of his would naturally lead his followers who were able to write to record his words in order to repeat them to those who clamoured to know what he had said; and there is nothing at all in any demonstrably early writing to suggest that such a practice would be distasteful to Muhammad. But it cannot be proved that any single tradition or group of traditions now extant were copied from the memoranda of the Companions. The most that can be said is that the canonical collections *may* preserve some such traditions.

Written hadith were, no doubt, objectionable to old-fashioned and orthodox traditionists, who preserved in their memories an enormous number of traditions and enjoyed no small reputation on that account. Objections, too, were raised by those who saw that in many points hadith were contradictory to the Quran. Those also who repeated traditions which were genealogically unsound and accounted unworthy of a place in the written, and soon to become, canonical collections could not but view the corpus of Bukhārī and his imitators with acute displeasure.

The basis of hadith is essentially religious, and during the Umayyad period theologians were under a cloud; so that it was not until the second century was well advanced that hadith of a religious character won their way into literature. Of course, a considerable number of traditions which were subsequently incorporated in the canonical collections of hadith were not committed to writing for the first time by the collectors. A goodly number of works on jurisprudence were already in existence besides the well-known works of Abū Ḥanīfa, Shaibānī, Shāfi'ī, and Abū Yūsuf.

The earliest date which Muhammadans give for the collection of hadith is contained in the following tradition, said to rest on the authority of Mālik b. Anas (94–179). 'Umar b. 'Abdu-l-'Azīz wrote to Abū Bakr. b. Muhammad b. 'Amr with the order: 'See what hadith of the prophet of God are extant or ancient customs (*sunna maḍīya*) or hadith known to 'Amra, and write them down; for I stand in dread of the disappearance of knowledge and of the death of them that possess it.' This Abū Bakr. b. Muhammad was one of the Anṣār whom 'Umar II appointed judge at Medina, and 'Amra was his aunt. Of the statement Sir William Muir writes[1]: 'About a hundred years after Muhammad, the Caliph 'Umar II issued circular orders for the formal collection of all extant tradition. The task thus begun continued to be vigorously prosecuted; but we possess no authentic remains of any compilation of an earlier date than the middle or end of the second century of the Hijra.' It would seem that this writer accepts the statement at its face value; but the fact that no authentic remains of this alleged first-century compilation are extant, and that the indefatigable students and compilers of tradition in the third century make no mention of an effort to trace such early documents, suggest very strongly that the tradition is not based on fact. It is difficult, if not impossible, to suggest a cogent reason why such an early collection, if it existed, should never have been mentioned by later scholars whose life-work it was to recover the genuine hadith of the apostolic period. For this reason the hadith must be regarded as an invention designed to connect the pious caliph, whose zeal for the sunna was gratefully recognized by theologians, with the tradition literature of Islam. This seems the more likely, as another tradition connects Ibn Shihāb Al Zuhrī with 'Umar II in this work. Moreover, Mālik's statement is only to be found in Al Shaibānī's recension of the Muwaṭṭa. It is absent from the other versions.

Two other second-century writers have been cited as authors of compilations of hadith, namely, 'Abd al Malik b. Juraij and Sa'īd b. Abī 'Arūba. Their works

[1] *Op. cit.*, pp. 33 f.

are not extant; but from the description of them given by later writers there is little doubt but that they were books of jurisprudence (*Fiqh*), drawn up with a view to stabilizing the sunna. Therefore they only incidentally contained traditions; their primary purpose was to serve as handbooks for lawyers. The need for such works increased when the free development of the public religious life of the community was no longer hindered by the worldly régime of the Umayyads.

Of a similar nature, though of far greater importance, is the *Muwaṭṭa* of Mālik b. Anas. This work, which has always been highly prized by Muhammadans, is not a collection of traditions. The author's interest was in jurisprudence, and his aim to establish a system of law based on the sunna of Medina. Thus he appeals to legal precedents as often as to hadith, which it was only incidentally his purpose to record for the sake of their legal significance. His object was not, like that of the later collectors, to ascertain what traditions of the prophet were current throughout the Muhammadan world and to test their authenticity by a series of artificial canons; but he had the severely practical and limited aim of establishing a system of law according to the agreement or consent (*ijmā'*) of the people of Medina. Thus he appeals, in matters in which his paragraphs coincide roughly with the hadith literature, not to hadith carried back by a chain of guarantors to the prophet, but to the sunna, which, with the legal decisions of recognized authorities and the consensus of opinion of the Medinotes, in his view constituted a system of law binding on the whole community. His method was to collect under distinct heads the sunna of Medina in regard to legal and religious matters: where tradition failed he appealed to *ijmāʿ*. Thus he had none of the theoretical interest in hadith which characterizes the traditionists of the next century. When necessary he did not hesitate to express his own opinion (*ray*) on difficult points where the evidence seemed to be at all dubious or self-contradictory. The following extract from the *Mudawwanāt* will best illustrate Mālik's method: 'Mālik was asked concerning certain persons who went raiding and disembarked in Cyprus, where they proceeded to buy sheep, honey, and butter, and paid for these articles with dinars and dirhems; Mālik disapproved. He further said to us of his own initiative: "I strongly object to coins which contain the mention of God and His book being taken and given to one that is unclean. I disapprove most strongly of such a practice." I asked him whether we might make purchases with dirhems and dinars of traders who disembarked on our coast, or of members of the tolerated cults. He replied that he disapproved. He was asked whether money might be changed by changers in Muslim markets who belonged to these cults. He replied that he disapproved.'[1]

That Mālik was no collector of traditions in the later sense is clear from his independent handling of his material. He does not always take care to trace back his *isnād*[2] or chain of guarantors to the prophet, nor are all the links in the chain set out. Thus, although his Muwaṭṭa saw the light a century before the canonical collections, it contains many hadith which have no place in the later works, because they

[1] x, p. 102, as quoted by Margoliouth, *Early Development of Muhammadanism*, p. 119.

[2] *Infra*, p. 23.

are not supported by a list of names reaching in uninterrupted succession from Muhammad to Mālik.

It is unfortunate for the study of Muhammadan origins that the extant versions of the text of the Muwaṭṭa differ so radically one from another. The explanation of these different versions is probably to be sought in the practice of Ijāza and Munāwala,[1] to which Mālik frequently resorted when pressed by a number of pupils.[2] The *textus receptus* of Mālik is the version of his Spanish pupil Yaḥyā b. Yaḥyā al Maṣmūdī; and it is this version which is commonly quoted as the Muwaṭṭa. But there are no less than fifteen other versions all differing from the Muwaṭṭa Yaḥyā and from each other. Of these by far the most important is the work of Muhammad b. Al Ḥasan Al Shaibānī, who was the pupil of Mālik and of Abū Ḥanīfa. This is generally cited as the Muwaṭṭa Muḥammad. It contains certain matter which is not to be found in the received text and has been worked over by Al Shaibānī and brought into accord with the tenets of his master Abū Ḥanīfa. In such cases he prefixes his own views and comments with the words 'Muhammad says'.[3]

The growing importance of tradition as an authoritative force in the establishment of the legal and ritual life of the community created a demand for hadith on every conceivable subject, a demand which, as will be seen in the following chapters, produced an unfailing

[1] See Additional Note to Chap. I.

[2] Cf. Sprenger in *ZDMG*, x, pp. 9 ff.

[3] A translation of a short section of the Muwaṭṭa illustrating the differences between the recensions of Yaḥyā and Shaibānī will be found in *MS*, ii, pp. 224–6.

supply; and naturally the vast accessions to current tradition thus generated necessitated some sort of systematic arrangement of material. The earliest collections are at one with the later in this, that attention was focused not on the *matn* or subject-matter of the tradition but on the *isnād* or chain of guarantors going back to a Companion of the prophet. The characteristic of the *Musnad*, the earliest type of collection, was that hadith, quite irrespective of their contents and subject-matter, were arranged under the name of the Companion on whose authority they were supported (*musnad*). The person who could repeat a respectable number of such *musnad* traditions received the honorific *Musnid*, or *Musnida* in the case of a woman. The *isnād* must always be in direct speech, thus: 'A told me, saying that B said C had informed him, saying D mentioned that he heard E relate, "I heard F ask the Apostle of God so and so."' The name *musnad*, which properly belonged to the individual tradition, passed over to the whole collection. A large number of such collections was current in the third century, though comparatively little of the literature survives to-day. The most important would seem to have been the *Musnad* of Aḥmad b. Ḥanbal. On account of its great bulk[1] this work was seldom to be found in its entirety even in antiquity. It contains about thirty thousand hadith grouped under the names of some seven hundred Companions. Though the author follows a plan of his own, dividing his work into books of traditions emanating from Muhammad's family, the Helpers, Women, and so on, he makes no

[1] The Cairene edition (1890) is in six volumes 4to, containing in all 2,885 pages.

attempt to group his gigantic store of tradition with any regard to the encyclopaedic range of the several subjects dealt with.

Aḥmad was an indefatigable Ṭālibu-l-'Ilm, and to his journeys we owe the *Musnadu-l-Shāmiyyīn* and other geographical groups of traditions. His vast collection was edited and published by his son 'Abd Allah Abū 'Abdu-l-Raḥmān (d. 290). The *Musnad* preserves a great many traditions which are not to be found elsewhere. Like all other collectors, Aḥmad practically always confined his criticism to the *isnād*; especially was he strict in his scrutiny of traditions from any one suspected of Qadarite leanings. *Post eventum* prophecies are to be found in the canonical collections; but not in the profusion and with the detail and exactitude of Aḥmad's collection. Hadith dealing with conquests, the geographical advantages of certain cities, and royal personages are the clearest examples of this development.

The *Musnad* is marked by a fearless indifference to the susceptibilities of the 'Abbāsids. Whereas the two great works of Bukhārī and Muslim may be searched in vain for any generous recognition of the merits of the Umayyads, Aḥmad, who forsooth had little to thank their successors for, preserves many of the numerous traditions extolling the glories of the Banū Umayya which must at one time have been current in Syria. A similar liberal attitude is adopted towards hadith which support the claims of the Shī'as. The great importance of this gigantic collection of tradition lies in its wealth of detail. Its value as a witness to events in the prophet's life, real and fictitious, is best illustrated in Margoliouth's *Muhammad*.

Later writers in the opposing schools often edited the collections of their leaders, arranging the authorities in alphabetical order, so that we read of the *Musnadu-l-Shāfi'i* or the *Musnadu-Mālik*. The reference is to the works mentioned on page 20 arranged as *musnads*. The word *musnad* is often misapplied by Muhammadan scholars, who speak of tradition works in general as *musnads*, e.g. of the *Musnadu-l-Bukhari*, where *Jāmi'* would be correct.

By the middle of the third century hadith had attained such importance as a means of determining the practice and beliefs of the community that a more practical collection and arrangement than the musnads became imperative. It was felt generally that hadith must be (*a*) brought into closer relation with jurisprudence, and (*b*) put on an unassailable footing. The controversy among the doctors of Islam which determined whether the community might develop its customs and re-interpret them according to the needs of each age, or whether it must rigidly conform to the practices and precedents of the apostolic generation, was probably responsible for the great impetus given to the collection and codifying of hadith. At this time traditions were written down with the definite aim of establishing an unerring authority for law and custom; thus, though the collectors devoted scrupulous attention to the *isnād*, so far as the arrangement of traditions was concerned the *isnād* was subordinate to the *matn*. Traditions were recorded according to their subject and the subject-matter was arranged under the headings of law books. Such collections were *Muṣannafāt*. The object of the *muṣannaf* was to provide the lawyer with a handbook of tradition in which he could readily look up the *ipsissima verba* of the prophet and thus silence an objector. The *musnads* were obviously unsuited to such a purpose: unless one knew the name of the original guarantor of a particular hadith one might have to read through the whole corpus of tradition to find it. While no ordered arrangement of oral and written tradition existed it was impossible to ask that young men who were being trained for the office of judge in the various provinces should be made to study hadith.

The task of the compilers was to demonstrate the practical value of hadith for the practical lawyer. The first and most important of the *Muṣannafs* is the *Ṣaḥīḥ*, 'the Genuine', of Abū 'Abd Allah Muhammad b. Isma'īl Al Bukhārī (194–256). This is a corpus of tradition pure and simple, compiled with the object of providing an orthodox criterion in all matters of jurisprudence.[1] The author applied himself to the task by adopting as the framework of his book headings which covered the whole range of *fiqh*. His work is divided into ninety-seven books, which again are divided into 3,450 *babs* or chapters. The traditions themselves are preceded by a *tarjama* or rubric designed to lead the reader to a decision where authorities in the various *Madhāhib* or schools differ. As Al Qasṭallānī has said, 'Bukhārī's *fiqh* is contained in the headings of his chapters.' The *tarjama* consists of a text from the Quran, or quite as often of a fragmentary hadith for which no *isnād* is

[1] As Chapter V will show, jurisprudence is by no means the only interest of hadith. Inasmuch as the Ṣaḥīḥ is a Jāmi' it contains *inter alia* historical, biographical, and eschatological matter. It is precisely its many-sided character which lends charm to the study of the hadith literature.

forthcoming. It is generally supposed that the author regarded these last as genuine, but was unable to find a genuine chain of transmittors. There is great acumen behind the selection of these texts and fragmentary traditions with which most chapters are furnished, for they suggest a connexion in thought and a consequent interpretation of a hadith which is otherwise neutral or susceptible of a contrary meaning. Moreover, in cases where the Quran was invoked the author appeared to have the support of an unimpeachable authority. An interesting feature of these paragraphs is that they sometimes occur without any hadith following. It has been inferred from this that although Bukhārī planned to cover the whole field of *fiqh* he sometimes failed to find confirmatory hadith and left the heading in the air, as it were, in the hope that the hiatus would some day be filled. This theory of the gaps is in keeping with the general purpose of this and other *musannafāt*, and accords with the scrupulous honesty and exactitude of the author himself. M. Houdas, however, makes the interesting suggestion [1] that they are in reality a polemic against the Murjiites: 'El-Bokhari . . . usa d'un moyen détourné pour atteindre plus sûrement l'hérésie qui menaçait l'existence même de l'islamisme; et, tandis que ses confrères se bornaient à classer et étiqueter leurs hadits, il songea à en faire une arme offensive contre les Mordjiites et contre tous ceux qui attentaient à la pureté primitive de la religion musulmane.' Thus he sees a peculiar significance and purpose in the first hadith recorded by Bukhārī, 'Works are only to be judged by their inten-

[1] *El Bokhari. Les Traditions islamiques traduites . . . par O. Houdas et W. Marcais*, ii, Paris, 1906, pp x ff.

tion,' and in the chapter on Faith. In his view, the explanation given above does not suffice. It is to be regretted that M. Houdas has not worked out his interesting theory in detail. It is not difficult to find examples to which his explanation could hardly apply. It might be held, for instance, that the first hadith, which continues, 'As for him who migrates to obtain worldly possessions or to marry, his migration will be rewarded according to its object,' is rather a protest against the usurpation of the term Muhājir than an attack on the Murjiites. Nevertheless, as M. Houdas well says: 'Quoi qu'il en soit de cette question bien secondaire en somme, El Bokhari a, d'une part, rendu un signalé service à l'islamisme en conjurant le péril Mordjiite, et, d'autre part, il a, pour ainsi dire, fixé d'une manière définitive la constitution pratique de la religion du Prophète.'

Tradition reports that this remarkable man took cognizance of 600,000 hadith,[1] and himself memorized more than 200,000. Of these he has preserved to us 7,397, or, according to other authorities, 7,295. If one adds to these the fragmentary traditions embodied in the *tarjama* the total is 9,082. On the other hand, the same tradition is often repeated more than once under different chapters (*Abwāb*), so that if repetitions are disregarded the number of distinct hadith is reduced to 2,762, which are to be found in the 3,450 *abwāb* into which his book is divided.[2] When one reflects

[1] Ibn Khallikān, *Wafayātu-l-A'yān*, ed. Wüstenfeld, p. 580. These figures must be taken with a grain of salt. It is hardly likely that a man of Bukhārī's ability would commit to memory 200,000 hadith in order to utilize less than a twentieth of them.

[2] I have taken these figures from Houdas, *op. cit.*

from these figures furnished by a Muslim historian that hardly more than one per cent. of the hadith said to be openly circulating with the authority of the prophet behind them were accounted genuine by the pious Bukhārī, one's confidence in the authenticity of the residue is sorely tried. Where such an enormous preponderance of material is judged false, nothing but the successful application of modern canons of evidence can restore faith in the credibility of the remainder. This is not, of course, to assert that the hadith literature is destitute of any historical foundation: such a conclusion would be unwarranted. But the undoubted historical facts do demand that each individual hadith should be judged on its merits.

So far as one is able to judge, Bukhārī published the result of his researches into the content of what he believed to be genuine tradition with all the painstaking accuracy of a modern editor. Thus he records even trifling variants in the hadith, and wherever he feels that an explanatory gloss is necessary either in *isnād* or *matn* it is clearly marked as his own. When a variant has been given he sometimes adds his comment at the end, *Qāla Abū ʿAbd Allah . . . ashbah*, in my opinion the words so and so are more probably correct. In the Appendix will be found a translation of the Kitābu-l-Qadar from this most important of all hadith collections.[1]

Though the text of the *Ṣaḥīḥ* does not present the unusual divergences in type to be found in the *Muwaṭṭa* it has survived in several recensions. It is only to be expected that a collection which, according to Ibn

[1] Reproduced, without critical and historical notes, from my article in *JRAS*, January 1924, by permission of the Society.

Khallikān,[1] was read before ninety thousand hearers, should now be extant in several different forms. Of these the best known is that founded on a critical edition made by Muhammad Al Yunīnī (d. 658). This was printed at Bulāq in 1314, is carefully vocalized, and contains marginal notes of variant readings. The commentary of Aḥmad b. Aḥmad Al Qasṭallānī (d. 923), *Irshādu-l-Sārī*,[2] is of such value as to be wellnigh indispensable. The version of Abū Dharr, represented by Krehl's text, is also of considerable value: it is frequently at variance with the received text.

Nothing is more eloquent of the exalted position of hadith in the Islamic community from the third century onwards, and of the prominent position of Al Bukhārī among the *Aṣḥābu-l-ḥadīth*, than the extravagant homage which was paid to him and his work. A man who laboured sixteen years on the compilation of his corpus, who sought the aid of prayer before committing a tradition to writing,[3] and who interrogated over one thousand shaikhs living in places so distant as Balkh, Merv, Nisapur, the principal towns of Mesopotamia, the Hijaz, Egypt, and Syria, deserved well of his co-religionists. If Muslims since his death have

[1] *Loc. cit.*

[2] Bulāq, 1305, ten vols. For the literature see Brockelmann, *Geschichte d. arabischen Litteratur*, i, pp. 158 ff.

[3] Bukhārī's work from first to last was an act of consummate piety. He was inspired to undertake the task, he says, by a dream in which he seemed to be driving away flies from the prophet's person. An interpreter of dreams told him that the flies were lies which had gathered round apostolic tradition. He never afterwards inserted a hadith in his collection until he had made an ablution and offered up a prayer of two *rak'as*.

canonized him, made pilgrimages to his tomb, and invoked his saintly aid in the difficulties of this life, they have but shown their devotion to the man who holds the position next their prophet. The latter, indeed, is reported to have been seen in a dream awaiting the arrival of Bukhārī at the gates of Paradise.[1]

Another *Muṣannaf* on which Islam has also conferred the title *Al Ṣaḥīḥ* is that of a younger contemporary of Bukhārī, Muslim b. Al Ḥajjāj (d. 261). Its contents are practically identical with Bukhārī's collection except in the *isnāds*, and the difference in treatment is really not very great. The principal difference is the absence of the paragraph headings characteristic of Bukhārī. Muslim's work is arranged according to *Fiqh*, but he does not follow his plan so scrupulously: thus, while Bukhārī often arranges the same tradition with a different *isnād* under different paragraphs when it is suitable to support more than one point of law and custom, Muslim places the parallel versions together. He does not plunge straightway into his task, but prefaces his book with a statement of the conditions a tradition must fulfil before it can be regarded as genuine and authentic.[2] Every hadith which could serve as a support for *fiqh* must itself rest upon the authority of men whose trustworthiness was above suspicion (*thiqāt*). Further, the authorities must stand in unbroken succession (*ittiṣāl*); it must be demonstrable that they were contemporaries, and were actually in personal intercourse. Such a hadith must contain the words *haddathanī*, *samiʿtu*, or some other

[1] Houdas, II, xxiii.

[2] Some extracts from his introduction will be found in Chap. IV.

word implying personal intercourse. Another category of hadith which was not so highly esteemed was called *mu'an'an*; in these in place of a verb of hearing or telling it is only asserted that A narrates from (*'an*) B. Muslim was willing to accept such hadith if it could be established that A and B were contemporaries, but Bukhārī demanded a further proof, that they should have been in personal contact: it was not sufficient that A should report—though in good faith—that B had related a certain hadith unless it could be proved that he himself had met him and therefore could be presumed to have heard it from his mouth, not through a third person. Muslim, however, excluded many traditions, not because he questioned their genuineness, but because they were not supported by *ijmā'*. His assertion of this prepared the way for a more thorough *Jāmi'*.[1]

The man Bukhārī has always been immeasurably greater in the popular estimation than Muslim, and the tendency has been for the work of the former to take precedence of the latter. The one is prized for its range over the whole field of *fiqh* and the strictness of the *shuruṭ* or rules for determining the trustworthiness of *rāwīs*, while the other is preferred for its more concise treatment of the material. Together they form an almost unassailable authority, subject indeed to criticism in details, yet deriving an indestructible influence from the *ijmā'* or general consent of the community in custom and belief, which it is their function to authenticate.

[1] It has not been considered necessary to give a translation of any section of Muslim's Ṣaḥīḥ, because the great majority of the hadith given in Ch. V are *muttafaq*, i. e. to be found in the *Ṣaḥīḥān*.

Besides these 'Two Genuine Books' there are four others which Islam has elevated to canonical rank, the whole being known as 'The Six Books' (*Al-kutubu-l-sitta*). These are the

Sunan of Abū Dāūd (d. 275).

Jāmi' of Abū 'Isā Muhammad al Tirmidhī (d. 279).

Sunan of Abū 'Abd Allah Muhammad b. Māja (d. 283).

Sunan of Abu 'Abd Al-Raḥmān al Nasā'ī (d. 303).[1]

The same motive which inspired Bukhārī moved the authors of the *Sunan* to their labours. Their aim was a narrower one, the compilation of a collection which would provide hadith dealing with all that was permissible and unpermissible to a Muslim. If so much genuine material had existed it is *a priori* inconceivable that it would have been passed over by Bukhārī and Muslim; consequently much greater latitude had to be given to all who narrated hadith that were desiderated. Apostolic authority was obtained for all the enactments in jurisprudence, but at the cost of a principle. Hadith which were only fairly sound *ḥasan* were included. As the author of *Maṣābīḥu-l-Sunna* tells us, 'support for most of the *aḥkām* comes from fair hadith'.

Abū Dāūd, a contemporary of Bukhārī, was a pupil of Aḥmad b. Ḥanbal, and the master of Al Nasā'ī. These two reversed the principle of the Ṣaḥīḥān that only hadith which rested on the authority of men universally esteemed trustworthy could be accepted, and they rejected only those which were universally

[1] These are loosely called 'the four sunnas', but inasmuch as Tirmidhī does not confine himself to matters of jurisprudence but deals with the whole field of hadith, his collection is properly a Jāmi'.

deemed unworthy of credence. They noted that some theologians were stricter than others in their scrutiny of the guarantors (*rijāl*), and where a favourable verdict had been accorded by a lenient scholar they accepted the hadith despite the weight of adverse criticism. At the same time they did not attempt to exalt the mass of additional matter to the same degree of respect as that accorded to a hadith admittedly ṣaḥīḥ. They expressed their opinion of the guarantors in no unmeasured terms. Abū Dāūd says that he wrote down half a million hadith, from which he selected 4,800; he calls these authentic, those which seem to be authentic, and those which are nearly so.[1]

The *Sunan* naturally fill up the gaps left by Bukhārī in his scheme of *fiqh*, and supply hadith in support of the most pettifogging details in the ritual and legal life of the community, a pedantry which threatened to bring the whole system of hadith into ridicule. Al Nasā'ī in his *Sunan*[2] takes notice of this ridicule.

Al Tirmidhī studied under Bukhārī, Aḥmad b. Ḥanbal, and Abū Dāūd. He was the first to classify the various hadith under the three headings *ṣaḥīḥ*, *ḥasan*, and *ḥasan ṣaḥīḥ*.

The great value of these *sunan* is in their witness to the extent to which the rival schools of Islam had established their ritualistic and legal systems in the third century. Al Tirmidhī in particular, with his wealth of inconsistent hadith, shows clearly how the

[1] Muir, *op. cit.*, xlii.

[2] Al Nasā'ī, Shāhdra 1282, i, p. 6, *qāla-l-mushrikūna innā narā ṣāhibakum yu'allimukum-l-kharā'ata.* In truth, what was really being said by men who objected to all the insignificant activities and even decencies of life being governed by apostolic tradition is here put into the mouth of the idolatrous contemporaries of Muhammad.

divergences in the orthodox schools of to-day were as clearly marked in his time.

Besides the 'six books' there were several other collections in circulation which failed to establish themselves in catholic consent. Of these the most important is that of Abū Muhammad 'Abd Allah al Dārimī (d. 255). The chief characteristic of his work is its eclectic and subjective method. He often records his own opinion as to whether a hadith is binding on the community or not; and he does not hesitate to give decisions contradicting earlier authorities. It is a little difficult to say whether his book is with propriety to be called *Sunan* or *Jāmi'*. It is in the main a manual of hadith necessary in jurisprudence, but it does not confine itself to purely legal matters. The author is indifferent to the minute questions of law and ritual so fully dealt with in the *Madhhab* collections of Abū Dāūd and Al Nasā'ī, so that even with the inclusion of matter of a general character his work is barely a third of the size of the other *sunan*. The tendency was for the pressure of the School (*Madhhab*) to increase, and a collection which failed to apply that pressure everywhere could not compete with *sunan* of a comprehensive character: thus Al Dārimī's work never won its way to canonical rank.

It would unduly prolong this work to enumerate and discuss other collections which enjoyed a certain amount of popularity, e.g. Baqī b. Makhlad Al-Qurṭubī (d. 276), Al 'Assāl (d. 349), which are sometimes quoted by writers with the encyclopaedic knowledge of Al Suyūṭī and Ibn Khaldūn. An account of them will be found in Brockelmann's *Geschichte*, and their hadith in some of the later compendia.

ADDITIONAL NOTE TO CHAPTER I.

Ijāza and Munāwala.

It will have been seen that the Ṣaḥīḥ of Bukhārī owed its existence to the arduous journeys undertaken by its author in search of hadith in circulation throughout the Muslim world. So great was the prestige of one who could narrate, as the last link in a chain, a tradition from the mouth of the prophet that those who were prevented by the responsibilities of life from undertaking these journeys in quest of *'ilm* had to find some other means to secure their admission to this apostolic succession. The means lay ready to hand. Mālik b. Anas had been known to give his pupils a written text with his authority to repeat its contents with the formula *ḥaddathana*, as though the conveyance had been by word of mouth. This process was called Munāwala, 'personal transmission' or 'handing over'. *Ijāza*, 'permission', was more lax. A teacher or *rāwī* was asked to allow a person to promulgate a collection of hadith in his name. Mālik is said to have allowed a pupil to do this without examining his text. The extraordinary differences between extant texts of the Muwaṭṭa are probably the sequel.

Bukhārī evidently felt some hesitation about traditions by way of munāwala; but in the following centuries, when the zeal of the 'Searchers after Knowledge' was at its height, *ijāza* could be given by letter or by proxy by an authority living in one end of the Muhammadan world to an applicant in the other. It would seem that when the content of tradition had been committed to writing, and partially established by *ijmā'*, the continued pursuit of 'knowledge' merely represented the activities of the credulous, who believed that there was still a residue of genuine apostolic tradition to be recovered, and who hoped to add their finds to the collections which had been accepted or were then winning their way to recognition in the second rank.

II

THE UMAYYAD PERIOD

Faint influence of the great Umayyad line on tradition.—Character and policy of their régime.—No fixed religious use.—Hostile attitude of doctors towards Umayyads reflected in hadith coined to influence the pious.—Official counter-invention of hadith.—Syrian hadith.—Hadith frankly recognized as inventions.

An account of the rise and character of the Umayyad dynasty would be naturally sought in a general history of the Caliphate rather than in a description of the traditions of Islam. But some explanation is certainly needed to show why Islam in its canonical literature has remained unmindful of the inestimable service rendered to its empire, and ungrateful for the enduring prestige bequeathed it by the Umayyads. The reason is that in authoritative tradition the voice of the schools of the Iraq and the Hijaz is to be heard sounding the praises of Abu Bakr, 'Umar, and 'Alī, and sometimes of 'Uthmān; but the Syrian tradition for the most part perished with its great dynasty.[1]

The compilation of the canonical collections dates from the time when the 'Abbasids were firmly in the saddle, and by this time systematic efforts had long been made to extirpate the memory of the predecessors of the reigning house. We know that the names of the Umayyads were even removed from public monuments.

[1] The Musnad Aḥmad, as we have seen, is an exception.

Earlier writers [1] have with good reason emphasized the godless régime of the Umayyads, yet it would be a mistake to regard it as entirely worldly. Lammens [2] has pointed out that after the time of 'Umar the public treasury, the army, booty of war, and the administration were called *māl Allāh*, *jund Allāh*, *fai Allāh*, and *sulṭān Allāh* respectively.[3] The Belgian savant gives good reason for his assertion that the religion of Yazīd, in the eyes of the orthodox the arch offender, was no better and no worse than that of his contemporaries. It has been recorded as a heinous offence that the Caliph Mu'āwiya sat down to pronounce the *Khuṭba* (solemn oration); yet this posture while giving public direction was common in the pre-Muhammadan era (*jāhiliyya*), and Muhammad is said in the canonical traditions to have sat down in the pulpit (*minbar*) while addressing the faithful. It is undoubtedly due to later writers' ignorance of the practice of antiquity that they explain the references to 'Uthman sitting in the *minbar* during the *khuṭba* to betrothals (*khuṭbatu-l-nikāḥ*).[4] Curiously enough in this matter, in which they have been held up to reproach as godless innovators, the Umayyads were adhering to the sunna of the prophet, and preserved the early significance of the *minbar* as the seat of judgement on which the ruler sat.[5] Only in the days

[1] E. g. Von Kremer and Dozy.

[2] *Études sur le règne du Calife Omaiyade Mo'awia Ier. Mélanges de la Faculté orientale*, Beyrout, 1906, p. 9.

[3] 'Expressions sonores, formules archaïques, demeurées pratiquement vides de sens,' *op. cit.*, vol. ii, p. 88.

[4] Jāḥiẓ Bayān, i. 50, and cf. *MS*, p. 53.

[5] There may have been a simpler explanation: Mu'āwiya in middle

of the next dynasty did the *minbar* degenerate into a pulpit from which the weekly sermon was delivered. Indeed, the role played by the mosque itself in the early days of the Islamic empire was radically different from that of later times. At first it served the purpose of a town hall or council chamber. The Umayyads took counsel with their advisers and transacted their public business in the mosque, not in their palaces. While still to a certain extent followers of the old democratic principle of tribal government, they were not slow to see the importance of the weekly harangue from the pulpit.

In some respects the Umayyad administration was far in advance of its time. It was marked by a genial tolerance of Christianity and other religions. One of Muʿāwiya's contemporaries protested that the Caliph would have employed negroes in public offices had it suited his purposes of state.[1] This reproach would not unnaturally follow Muʿāwiya's treachery in employing a Christian physician to rid him of the powerful Abdu-l-Raḥmān, the son of the great general Khālid, 'the sword of Allah', whom he feared as the rival of his son Yazīd. He even allowed the said Christian to collect religious imposts from the people of Homs. Tolerance of Christians was not confined to Syria. The governor of Medina actually employed Christians from Aila (Aqaba) to police the holy city.[2] In the Iraq, too, they held offices of importance.

A variety of reasons led to this toleration of

age was gluttonous and corpulent. *Al Fakhrī*, ed. Cairo, 1317, pp. 98 ff.

[1] Al Fakhri, *ib.*

[2] Despite their provocative function there is no record of any protest having been made against their presence.

Christians: first, there were the aristocratic connexions of the Christians among the Arabs of the peninsula; the kingdom of Ghassan, and the names of Bakr, Taghlib, and the Banū Ḥanīfa, all co-religionists, stood high in the estimation of Arabians. Secondly, Islam had not hardened into a systematized religion; and owing to the poll-tax on *dhimmis*, or members of tolerated religions, an increase of converts meant a decrease in revenue. And thirdly—perhaps the most potent reason—the Syrians, who formed such a powerful and important part of the Umayyad armies, were Christianized Arabs who cared little for Islam. Ibnu-l-Faqih[1] calls them *muslimūna fī akhlāqi-l-Naṣārā*, Muslims with the characteristics of Christians. It was not uncommon at this time for a soldier in the Caliph's army to ring the bell of a neighbouring church, or perform other minor duties of a religious nature among the Christian community.[2]

These examples of the relations between Muslims and *dhimmis* in the Umayyad period will illustrate how utterly different in outlook were the caliphs and the theologians.[3] It could hardly be said that an enormous number of *soi-disant* Muslims flouted the sunna: they were simply ignorant of its existence.

In the wars that seem inevitably to follow the rise of a new religion it is often difficult to separate their political from their religious significance. And it is

[1] 315, 9 (*Bibl. Geog.*, ed. M. de Goeje).

[2] 'Devenus musulmans, moitié par ambition, moitié par lassitude, ils constataient sans regret l'attachement de leurs parents et de leurs femmes à l'ancienne religion,' *op. cit.*, p. 54.

[3] Mālik's attitude towards the tolerated cults as illustrated on p. 21 above is an instructive contrast.

highly probable that much of the odium that has gathered round the Umayyad name in the sphere of religion is really due to their determination to hold the pre-eminence in temporal affairs. Their natural enemies, as later events so clearly proved, were in the Hijaz and the Iraq; and consequently the traditionists in these territories who claimed to interfere in the public and private lives of the subjects of the Syrian monarchs were repressed with scant ceremony.

It can hardly be denied that the policy of the Umayyads—always with the exception of the piously brought up 'Umar b. 'Abdu-l-'Azīz—was dictated by considerations of a worldly rather than a religious nature. They had practically no interest in religious law, and no great veneration for the teaching of the prophet. The *Book of Songs* is an eloquent witness to the unbridled licence of thought and life at that time. Al Walīd II, when threatened with the divine wrath pronounced in the Quran against the enemy of religion, actually threatened to use the sacred volume as a target for his arrows.

However, it must always be borne in mind that the sources from which our knowledge of this period is gained are for the most part marked by a fierce hatred of the Umayyads and all their works; so that those who denounce them as the enemies of the faith shut their eyes to the wise and firm administration of the early rulers of that house, their conquests, military organization, navy, and public works. All these benefits were as nothing in the sight of their pharisaical subjects in Medina. Like the Ḥasīdīm of old, who held fast to Law and Tradition, standing aloof from the national party and its materialistic aims, the doctors of Medina refused to deal with the caliphs of Damascus. They laboured to establish the sunna of the community as it was, or as it was thought to have been, under the prophet's rule, and so they found their bitterest enemies in the ruling house. As sincere Muslims they risked their lives by refusing to do homage to the Umayyads; and it required the ferocity of the notorious Al Ḥajjāj to compel them to yield even lip service to his masters so deeply were their religious sentiments outraged. The consequences of the attitude of the government were twofold. In the first place, abysmal ignorance of even the rudiments of Islam prevailed over the Muslim world; and in the second place, a theoretical turn was given to the subterranean labours of scholars who were endeavouring to elaborate a rule of life and thought for the community. Debarred by the policy of the Umayyads from any share in the administration—good orthodox Muslims who accepted office under the worldly régime were scathingly rebuked by the godly irreconcilables—their work suffered under the disadvantage inseparable from all legislation which is not founded on, and tested by, experience. They were as it were legislating for posterity, and much that was idealistic and out of relation to everyday life was incorporated in their work to serve as a basis for the normal practice of the future.

How far the surprising ignorance of the ordinary duties and beliefs of a Muslim which reigned throughout a large part of the Muslim world towards the end of the first century is due to the policy of the Umayyads, and how far a fanatical desire to proselytize has wrongly been attributed to the earlier Muhammadans, are points for the historian to pronounce upon. But certain it is that at this time the people of Basra did not know the rules of ritual prayer. Al Bukhārī tells us[1] how Malik b. Al Huwairith instructed the people there in the postures proper to prayer. The *tarjama* is interesting in that it contemplates the giving of formal instruction in ritual. Further, the existence in Syria of a salutation Al-salām ʿalā ʾllah shows that the chapter devoted by traditionists to the correct forms of greetings and salutations was by no means uncalled for.

The contrast between the theoretical and the practical at the end of the first century is startling. For in theological circles, if Al Dārimī is to be believed, the sunna was declared to be the judge of the Quran, not vice versa.[2] This view was shared by Al Shaibānī and Al Shāfiʿī, and theologians did not shrink from proclaiming as a dogma the corollary that the sunna was of divine origin.

Amid general ignorance and indifference pious doctors painfully gathered material for a reconstruction of the conditions of Muhammad's time. They questioned all living Companions and Followers on points of law and custom. Driven by a deep sense of religious obligation to gather the precious material at any cost to themselves, these men did not shrink from travelling thousands of miles in search of Companions who could give them first-hand information of the prophet's actions. Thus armed with the authority of the prophet, the traditionists hoped, by giving the

[1] Adhan, no. 45; Krehl, i, p. 175.

[2] I hesitate to put an obelus to a tradition which Goldziher (*MS*, ii, p. 21) accepts.

widest possible circulation to hadith, to rouse the public to a sense of their religious duties, and to undermine the world power of the government. The temptation to use so potent a weapon to further their political aims was more than flesh and blood could resist. We may detect covert attacks on the Umayyad dynasty in the numerous hadith which extol the merits of the prophet's family, whose representatives were, of course, the house of Ali.

The hadith literature faithfully reflects the passions roused by the government. The burning question was how the believer was to conduct himself under a godless tyranny. Was it a duty to take up arms against the tyrant, or must his rule be accepted as ordained by God? There was a party which refused to have anything to do with the Umayyads, who declined to take office under them, who reviled them and their vice-gerents, their generals, and their ignoble instruments the forgers of prophetic traditions, and who promised the martyr's crown to him who died in resisting the oppressor. Traces of this attitude still survive in the canonical collections in hadith like the following: 'A Muslim must hearken and obey whether he approves or dislikes an order so long as he is not commanded to disobey God. In that case obedience is not incumbent on him.' Again, 'No obedience is due where disobedience to God is involved. Obedience is only due to lawful demands.'

The Murjiites, on the other hand, refused to see in the suppression of religious law any cause for refusing homage to the Umayyads; it sufficed for them that their rulers were nominally Muslims: they did not care to inquire too closely into their actions. A good example, directly contradictory in import to the last two, is: 'Whoso obeys me obeys God. Likewise whoso disobeys me disobeys God. Whoso obeys an Amīr obeys me, and whoso disobeys an Amīr disobeys me. Verily an Imām is a shield behind which one fights and is protected. If he gives orders in the fear of God and with justice he will have his reward; if contrary thereto he will suffer for it.'[1] All three hadith are *muttafaq*.[2] These were the men who by lending themselves to the government as instruments in the promulgation of hadith favourable to the powers that be did so much to keep down the rising tide of disaffection.

But it was the intermediate party which left the deepest mark on the hadith literature and on the thought of Islam. They did not go so far as the Murjiites, who boggled not at supporting even the massacre of the pious, but they taught that though a ruler was the most unworthy of men, it was wrong to take up arms against him to the detriment of the state and the unity of Islam. 'Hearken and obey though an Abyssinian slave be made your governor with a head like a dried grape!' They preached the duty of submission to the will of God, and of patience and endurance under oppression. 'Let him who dislikes the conduct of his Amīr be patient; for he who divides the Muslim community a hand's breadth shall die the death of a pagan.' At all costs the unity of Islam must be preserved. Muslim gives the following on

[1] The text of the Mishkat varies between *minhu* and *munnata*. The commentators prefer the former, and explain *'alaihi minhu: 'alaihi wizran thaqīlan min ṣanī'ihi*.

[2] See Glossary of Technical Terms.

the authority of 'Arfaja: 'Evil times will come repeatedly. But he who seeks to separate this people which is a united community slay him with the sword be he who he may.' Hadith of a similar import are extremely numerous. The attitude of acquiescence was supported by the doctrine of ijmā', an example from the first century of that respect which Islam has always paid to the *fait accompli*. Invariably in times of stress the theologian and would-be reformer appealed to it to deliver him from an impossible position, and never in vain.

Most probably the prolific output of pseudo-prophetic hadith had their origin in the days of the Umayyad oppression. The pious, in the name of Muhammad, who by projecting himself into an unhappy future becomes a *laudator temporis acti*, pronounce condemnation on the degeneracy of the times. 'The best age for my community was the time when I was sent, then the time following, then will arise a people whose word none can trust.' This hadith exists in very many different forms and collections. The following from Ibn Ḥanbal is of interest as showing the interpretation given to it in the time of the next dynasty: 'Prophecy will be with you as long as God wills; then he will take it away; then will come a caliphate on the pattern of prophecy; then will come a tyrannical[1] kingdom . . . then will come a kingdom in arrogance: then will come a caliphate on the pattern of prophecy. Then the prophet was silent. Ḥabīb said: When 'Umar b. 'Abdu-l-'Azīz came to the throne I wrote to him

[1] '*āḍḍan* explained by the commentator *ya'aḍḍu ba'ḍu ahlihi ba'ḍan ka'aḍḍi-l-kilāb*, 'its subjects will bite one another after the manner of dogs'.

informing him of this hadith, and said: "I hope that you are to be the Amīru-l-Mūminīn after the tyrannical and arrogant reigns," whereat he was much pleased.' This hadith is reported by Hudhaifa, who is credited elsewhere with being the prophet's confidant on eschatological matters.[1] His information from this source is asserted to extend to the *yaumu-l-qiyāma*, so that, for the orthodox, there is an adequate explanation of the prophecies on such matters as the rise of the Turks and the principal battles fought against the Byzantines.

The reigning house could not afford to leave their opponents with the sole right of collecting and promulgating hadith: in fact, Ṭabarī[2] states that Mu'āwiya I ordered that all hadith favourable to the house of 'Alī should be suppressed, and the glories of the family of 'Uthmān be extolled in hadith. The Umayyad hand is perhaps most clearly seen in the traditions which were forged to emphasize the sanctity of Jerusalem *vis-à-vis* Mecca and Medina. While his rival 'Abd Allah b. Zubair was in possession of the holy places, and could bring pressure to bear upon the pilgrims who resorted thither, and seduce them from their allegiance to the northern house, the problem which confronted 'Abdu-l-Malik in Syria was not unlike that of Jeroboam the son of Nebat in those regions; nor was his countermove dissimilar. Whereas Jeroboam provided within his own territory sanctuaries for the veneration of his subjects, 'Abdu-l-Malik hit upon the expedient of enjoining a pilgrimage to the mosque he built in Jerusalem instead of the orthodox journey to Mecca and Medina. All that was necessary was to declare

[1] See Bab Fitan and the *locus classicus* in Qadar, p. 173.

[2] ii, p. 112.

that a circumambulation of the holy place at Jerusalem possessed the same validity as that enjoined at Mecca, and to procure for his assertion a confirmatory hadith with an *isnād* going back to the prophet himself.[1] 'Journey only to three mosques, Al Masjidu-l-Ḥarām, the mosque of the prophet, and the mosque of Jerusalem,' is the form this tendentious hadith takes in Al Bukhārī.[2] The inventor is Al Zuhrī, who fathers it on Abū Huraira. This was countered from Medina by the following hadith, which comes next in Bukhārī's *bab*: 'A prayer in this my mosque is better than a thousand prayers in others, except the Masjidu-l-Ḥarām.' The interesting feature of these two hadith as Bukhārī records them lies in the *tarjama*, which reads: 'Of the superiority of prayer in the *mosques of Mecca and Medina*.' Bukhārī was too scrupulous to omit from his collection a hadith which was supported by witnesses whose bona fides he did not suspect; but by the simple expedient of ignoring the references to the Masjidu-l-Aqṣā he asserted the paramount sanctity of the holy places of the Hijaz. Ibn Māja gives the Syrian version of the latter half of the second hadith—undoubtedly the original, since Muhammad in the Quran had established the sanctity of the Hijaz temples—to the effect that prayer at Jerusalem is a thousand times more effective than at other places.[3]

Many hadith which exalt the honour and sanctity of Syria over the rest of the Muslim world still find a place in some of the collections. Thus in Aḥmad's Musnad and the Jāmi' of Al Tirmidhī[4] we read that

[1] *Journal Asiatique*, 1887, p. 482.

[2] *Bab Faḍli-l-Ṣalāt*, Krehl, p. 299.

[3] *Sunan*, Delhi, p. 102.

[4] *Mishkātu-l-Maṣābīḥ*, p. 574.

the prophet said: 'Blessed be Syria! "Why?" we asked. "Because", said he, "the angels of the Compassionate spread their wings over it."' Abū Dāūd from 'Abd Allah b. 'Amr: 'There will be migration after migration and the best of men (will flee) to Abraham's place of refuge.' Again, Ibn Ḥawala: 'It will come to pass that armies will be assembled in Syria, the Yaman and Iraq.' Said he: 'Choose for me my course, O Apostle of God, if I live till that epoch.' He replied: 'Get you to Syria, for that land is chosen by God from his (whole) earth, and thither will he gather the chosen of his creatures. If you refuse (to go there) then get you to Yaman and water your flocks from its pools. Verily God hath guaranteed to me the safety of Syria and its people.'[1] Other hadith tell us that the prophet especially recommended Damascus as a place of residence, and appointed a suburb, Al Ghūṭa, a military rendezvous.

Another form of the Umayyads' official propaganda was the publication of hadith glorifying the name of the murdered 'Uthmān. He is said to have been marked out for the caliphate by the prophet, to have been a martyr, and destined to be the companion of Muhammad in paradise. The long and involved explanations of 'Uthmān's cowardice at Uhud and Badr,[2] which earned him the title Al Farrār, The Fugitive, are undoubtedly an attempt to defend the

[1] Most of the hadith that follow are quoted from the *Mishkat*, and can easily be found under the appropriate chapter headings. A more precise reference will not be given, for the reasons explained in the preface.

[2] *Manāqib 'Uthmān* in the various collections, and Houdas, ii, 600 f.

memory of one from whom the Umayyads claimed their right to the throne.

If any external proof were needed of the forgery of tradition in the Umayyad period, it may be found in the express statement of Al Zuhrī: 'These princes have compelled us to write hadith.'[1] Undoubtedly the hadith exalting the merit of the pilgrimage to the qubbatu-l-Sakhra at Jerusalem is a survival of the traditions Al Zuhrī composed. Ibn 'Aun, who died in the middle of the second century, refuses to credit traditions resting on the authority of Shahr b. Haushab because he had held office under the government.[2] It is difficult to imagine a more telling accusation. Al Bukhārī a century later feels no compunction in including traditions in Shahr's name in the category of 'genuine', presumably because he knew little or nothing about the circumstances of the time in which Shahr lived, nor the pressure that was brought to bear upon him. And it is to be remembered that Shahr is by no means the only Muḥaddith whose name appears both in the canonical collections of tradition and in the roll of Umayyad state officials.[3]

It need cause no surprise that comparatively few traditions 'inspired' by the Umayyad house survive. We have seen that a great many were in circulation while the dynasty flourished, and we hardly need the express assurance that the Abbasids sternly repressed them. The house of Abbas had ruled for more than a century when the great written collections were made, and during this time the theologians and muḥaddithūn

[1] Sprenger, *loc. cit.*, and Muir, *LM*, p. xxxiii.

[2] Al Tirmidhī (Bulaq, 1292, ii, p. 117), who constantly quotes hadith guaranteed by Shahr. The *Musnad* of Al Ṭayālisī, Ibn 'Aun's pupil, contains but three such.

[3] *MS*, pp. 40 ff.

had been able to develop their doctrines and practices without the hindrance, and often with the help, of the government. In these circumstances it would be astonishing if more than a faint trace of traditions favourable to the irreligious race of the Umayyads was allowed to appear. As a matter of fact, we find that those preserved by Al Bukhārī suggest to the faithful that Muʿāwiya was careless, or at all events eccentric, in his religious exercises. The following example must suffice: 'Muʿāwiya made an odd number of rakʿas after the evening prayer while a freed man belonging to Ibnu-l-ʿAbbās was present. Whereupon the freed man came and told his former master, who said: "Let him alone, for he has been in the society of the prophet of God."'[1]

There is a pathetic ring about the tradition ascribed by Aḥmad b. Ḥanbal to Shuraiḥ b. ʿUbaid. He says: 'The Ahlu-l-Shām were mentioned in Ali's presence with the remark "Curse them, O commander of the Believers." "No," said he, "for I heard the apostle of God say: The Abdāl are in Syria. Now they are forty men; when one dies God puts another in his place. By them rain is obtained,[2] victory gained over

[1] *Bāb Dhikr Muʿāwiya*, no. 28; Krehl, p. 446.

[2] Cf. Aghani, x (quoted *MS*, ii, p. 381 note) of Abdu-l-Malik: *Khalīfati-llāhi yustasqā bihi-l-maṭaru*. The Abdāl were an order of wonder-working saints who mingled unrecognized and often unperceived among their fellow-creatures. They formed the third of five orders of a mysterious hierarchy, at whose head stood the Quṭbu-l-Ghauth. See *Arabian Society in the Middle Ages*, Lane, London, 1883, pp. 47–9. On rain-making among the heathen Arabs, see Wellhausen, *Reste arabischen Heidentums*, p. 157. I suspect the activities alluded to here are similar to those of Rabbi Honi in the Talmud, *Taʿanith*, fol. 19 a.

our enemies, and punishment turned aside from the people of Syria."' This hadith is to be connected with the ritual cursing of the Umayyads. Al Ma'mūn had to send round a street-crier to threaten all those who spoke well of Mu'āwiya, and a collection of hadith assailing the honour and prestige of the Umayyads was circulated by Al Mu'tadid with the order that the cursing of the first of that dynasty should form part of the ritual. The presence of traditions of this kind in the Musnad of Ibn Ḥanbal strongly suggests that it was not only his theology but also his political fearlessness which made him an object of Al Ma'mun's hatred.

An account of the criticism which Muhammadans have from time to time passed on the hadith literature has been reserved for a later chapter; but it may not be out of place to examine the defence implicit in many of the hadith themselves. During a long period of suppression the pious had to endeavour to form the religious life of the community. They had no official position under the government—with few exceptions—and the prophet's position as the seal of the prophets and the revealer of the will of God for all time effectually shut the door to any fresh revelation. Thus those who desired to secure universal recognition of their dogmas must perforce cast them into a form which would be regarded as authoritative by the community. There was only one way of doing this, namely, to throw the teaching it was desired to inculcate into the form of a hadith with an *isnād* reaching back to the prophet. Second-century writers make no secret of this method. They recognize that it is only the form adopted to secure the respectful attention of their audience; they recognize, too, that it is a form adopted by all who wish to gain a respectful hearing from the piously disposed. Thus a hadith which obviously has no greater authority than those it seeks to undermine says: 'After my death sayings attributed to me will multiply just as a large number of sayings are attributed to the prophets who were before me. What is told you as a saying of mine you must compare with the Quran. What is in agreement therewith is from me whether I have actually said it or not.' This is but another way of saying that provided an invented hadith is edifying or unobjectionable to the orthodox, none need trouble to inquire whether it actually proceeded from the mouth of the prophet or not. Whatever the effect this frank admission may have on our estimate of the genuineness of the Muhammadan traditions as a whole, there is no necessity to impute the worst motives to these men who adopted the only course open to them to persuade their co-religionists. It is instructive to observe that the defence of the legitimacy of those who, according to Old Testament critics, promulgated a code of laws in the name of Moses some five hundred years after his death is in substance the same as that in the hadith last quoted.[1]

[1] 'To this conclusion, that Deuteronomy was written in the age of either Manasseh or Josiah, it is objected that the book plainly produced its effect on account of the authority which it was believed to possess, in other words, on account of its claiming, and being supposed, to be the work of Moses: if Josiah had not believed the ancient law-book of Israel to have been discovered, would he have attached any weight to its words? . . . Its force must have been due principally to the name of Moses, which it bore; and if the prophets were aware that it did not really possess his authority, then not only are they guilty of an act questionable morally, but the course taken

Less than half this space of time lay between the Muhammadan traditionists and their apostle. Moreover, the principle is canonized in Judaism, for we read in the Talmud a statement of startling similarity to that quoted above: 'Anything that a disciple of the wise may say in the future was revealed to Moses on Sinai.' The use here of the word *ḥaddesh* = *ḥaddatha* is extremely interesting and suggestive: the intimate relationship between the Talmud and some sections of the hadith literature is a subject to which I shall recur in another place.

In spite of these warning notes which still sound in

by them is a confession of moral impotence and failure: they resort to an external name to accomplish what centuries of their own teaching had failed to effect.

'In estimating these objections, it must be remembered firstly, that what is essentially new in Deuteronomy is not the *matter*, but the *form*. . . . Such laws as are really new in Deuteronomy are but the logical and consistent development of Mosaic principles. . . . All Hebrew legislation, both civil and ceremonial, however, was (as a fact) derived ultimately from Moses, though a comparison of the different Codes in the Pentateuch shows that the laws cannot all in their present form be Mosaic: the Mosaic nucleus was expanded and developed in various directions, as national life became more complex, and religious ideas matured. Nevertheless, all Hebrew laws are formulated under Moses' name,—a fact which shows that there was a *continuous Mosaic tradition* embracing a moral, a ceremonial, and a civil element: the new laws, or extensions of old laws, which as time went on were seen to be desirable, were accommodated to this tradition, and incorporated into it, being afterwards enforced by the priestly or civil authority as the case might be. . . . It is no fraudulent invocation of the legislator's name: it is simply another application of an established custom.'—S. R. Driver, *A Critical and Exegetical Commentary on Deuteronomy*, Edinburgh, 1902, pp. lv–lvii. All this is equally true of Muhammadan legislation and the ethical and moral truths inculcated in the hadith literature.

the hadith literature, there does not appear to have been any attempt to investigate the claims of any tradition to represent the actual words of Muhammad. Even Bukhārī was content to confine himself to a criticism of the genealogy of the isnād rather than the subject-matter of the tradition and the circumstances in which the guarantors lived, so that any tradition which could clothe itself in a canonical dress became *ipso facto* respectable.

III

THE ABBASID PERIOD

Character and policy of their régime.—Dynastic hadith, Alid Umayyad and Abbasid.—Shīa Collections.—Establishment of the sunna.—Talabu-l-'Ilm and its object.—Enormous growth of tradition.—Contradictions, critics and harmonizers.—Doctrine of Ijmā' applied to hadith.

A CONTEMPORARY would probably have noticed no difference between the lives of the Caliphs of Baghdad in their harems and banqueting-halls and the similar institutions of their deposed rivals in Damascus. *Wein, Weib und Gesang* might have been written over all alike. The great difference, which has profoundly influenced the subsequent course of Islam, was in their official attitude towards religious institutions. The 'Abbāsid could drink the forbidden wine as long and deeply as the Umayyad. But whereas the latter tolerated wine booths in the mosques, the former took pains to enforce his subjects' obedience to the Prophet's prohibition of wine with all the power of an oriental despot. Within their palaces the early monarchs of this line lived the lives which in the pages of the *Arabian Nights* still fire the imagination and form the stock-in-trade of the modern *rāwī*, and the legendary records of their carousals are probably better known in the Occident than any other Arabic work. But the 'Abbāsids understood their subjects well enough to perceive that if they made the revival of the sunna an integral part of their policy, and in their official capacity as Imāms conformed to the national religion, no serious interference with their personal tastes would ensue. Theoretical discussions of religious questions were popular amongst the most worldly princes in the halcyon days of the 'Abbāsid caliphate. Their bid for the support of the orthodox party was successful because of their avowed zeal for the sunna of the prophet. They wore his mantle (*burda*) on solemn state occasions to strengthen the idea that there was something sacrosanct in their authority; and honorifics which suggested that they were the true successors of the prophet and even his representatives were eagerly accepted by them, especially by the later caliphs.[1] Indeed, it may be said in general that as their political power declined, so their preoccupation in purely religious matters and their claim to religious authority increased.

During the Umayyad régime foreign converts had claimed in vain the equality which the prophet assigned to all Muslims. The Umayyad and the nobles of Syria openly treated all foreigners as subordinate to free-born Arabs. One of the consequences of this racial pride was that the more ambitious and unscrupulous foreigners pretended that they were of pure Arab descent, discarded their foreign names, and produced forged pedigrees tracing their descent to men famous in the sagas of Arabia. Especially among the more intellectual Persians, with their age-long traditions of culture and civilization, was there fierce resentment of the Arab domination, a fact which explains their

[1] Such titles as Amīnu-llah and Khairu-l-Quraish were given to their predecessors.

enthusiastic adoption of the Abbasid cause. With the accession of the new dynasty their chance had come. The tables were turned, and henceforth it was the comparatively ignorant Arab who was to be an object of ridicule to those he had formerly despised. Practically all the Abbasid viziers were Persians, or, at any rate, non-Arabs; and the caliphs, for the most part, made no secret of their preference for Persians. The results of this more liberal policy towards foreigners were manifold. It was responsible for the great impetus given to the study of philosophy and science through the medium of translations into Arabic of classical and Syrian writers, and for the increased knowledge of the Old and New Testaments, especially in regard to their eschatological and historical matter.

Though, as we have seen, there was a systematic attempt during the Abbasid caliphate, when the canonical collections of traditions were compiled, to root out all hadith favourable to the Umayyads, the voice of the Arab has not been altogether stilled. We seem to hear the despairing cry of the orthodox Arab of Medina in the tradition which Bukhārī records as spoken by the dying 'Umar to 'Abd Allah b. 'Abbās, the ancestor of the dynasty of that name, 'Praise be to God, who has not let me die by the hand of a Muslim. You and your father would gladly have seen Medina full of barbarians.' Now Al 'Abbās had more foreign slaves than any one else in the city.[1] This tradition is the more pointed in its application in that the assassin of 'Umar was a Persian. There is, too, a story of how Al 'Abbās excited the prophet's contempt

[1] *Faḍāilu-l-Aṣḥāb.*

by his cupidity and avarice, faults with which the true Arab had no sympathy. Its presence in Bukhārī's collection is a tribute to the fearless spirit of the collector.[1]

The Abbasids were keenly alive to the importance of the principle of the divine right of kings, the more so as their claim to the caliphate by right of inheritance was a principle foreign to the tribal customs of Arabia and one which Islam had never admitted. The court poet who could write some telling verses on the claim of the prophet's uncle as against that of his cousin, or attack the principle condemned in the Salic Law, could thereafter enjoy a life of ease. In hadith inspired by the Abbasids the Hashimite line was represented as sharing, by virtue of the revelation in Sura 8. 42, in the distribution of booty to the next-of-kin.[2] In Abū Dāūd's version of the story the significance of the hadith is underlined, for it is expressly stated that the Umayyads received nothing.

Muslim doctors never recognized the principle of a hereditary caliphate. Bukhārī's chapter on inheritances with the *tarjama*, 'We leave no inheritance. What we leave is alms,'[3] asserts the principle that the prophet had no heir in no less than five entirely different hadith. The principle which gave his power to the caliph was the *ijmā'u-l-umma*, the consent of the

[1] *Kitābu-l-Jizya*, no. 4; Krehl, ii, p. 294; and cf. *ib.*, i, p. 116, *Kitābu-l-Ṣalāt*, no. 42, for a variant of the same tradition.

[2] Bukhari, *Manāqib*, no. 3.

[3] For the extremely clever alteration in the Shī'a interest of the words lā nūrith mā taraknā ṣadaḳa into lā yūrath mā taraknā ṣadaqatan (What we leave as alms is not to be inherited) by the change of one letter and the cognizance taken of this in later versions of the text see *MS*, ii, pp. 103–4.

community. As a matter of fact, logic demanded the denial of a hereditary overlordship; for that would involve the assumption that the three first caliphs—the *khulafāu-l-rāshidūn*—were usurpers, and the admission either that right lay with the Alides or that the community had erred in accepting the Umayyads. A claim to the caliphate on the score of prophetic descent was a double-edged weapon, and one which the Alides were obviously more comfortable in handling.[1] The latter never ceased to maintain their right. An enormous number of traditions were forged to further Abbasid interests, some of which are pseudo-prophetic, as for instance that quoted by Al Suyūṭī,[2] 'The prophet said to 'Abbās: "In you shall rest prophecy and sovereignty."' There was an immense volume of this kind of tradition which need not be quoted. The author of the *History of the Caliphs* evidently did not prize such hadith highly, for he tells us that one to the effect that the prophet clothed 'Abbās and his son in his mantle, praying for a special blessing on them, together with the one just quoted is the best of those alleged to foretell the exaltation of the family of 'Abbās.

'Every corner of Irak and Hijaz was ransacked for traditions in support of the right of the house of Abbas. The doctors of law were required to formulate the principles of orthodoxy in explicit terms: and gradually the grand superstructure of the Sunnī church was raised on the narrow foundations of Abasside self-

[1] Professor Margoliouth remarks that in the earliest appointments of Caliphs relationship to the Prophet seems to have been a determining factor. Mu'āwiya was a brother-in-law.

[2] *Tārīkhu-l-Khulafā*, tr. Jarrett, p. 13.

interest,' says the Sayyid Amīr 'Alī.[1] Al Suyūṭī mentions a hadith in which the names of no less than six caliphs appear as guarantors of its contents.

However, despite the efforts of the Abbasids, the Muhammadan doctors never gave way on the general question. The caliphate was not an heirloom. They affirmed again and again that the dignity of the prophet was exclusively confined to Muhammad, and no one could possibly inherit it. But their peculiar consideration for the unique prophetic character of Muhammad did not result, as one might have expected, in the suppression of hadith favourable to the claims of the 'Alids. This was due partly to veneration for 'Alī and his family as martyrs, and partly to the fact that in the first centuries the Shī'as were not schismatics, nor a body of people held together by doctrine or political aims. At most they desired to see the triumph of the house of 'Alī, and gave their support to any movement which would tend to further this project. Thus it is that the canonical collections abound in stories extolling the memory of 'Alī. Yet there is no yielding when the prophetic office is involved. 'Were there a prophet after me it would be 'Umar b. Al Khaṭṭāb.'[2] Many of them were collected and summarized by Al Suyūṭī, of which the following are examples[3]: 'O God, befriend the friend of 'Alī and oppose his enemy. 'Alī is part of me and I of 'Alī.'

[1] *The Spirit of Islam*, Calcutta, 1902, p. 287.

[2] lau kāna ba'dī nabiyyun lakāna 'Umara b. Al Khaṭṭāb. The compiler of the Mishkāt adds rawāhu Al-Tirmidhī waqāla hādha ḥadīthun gharīb. 'This from the collection of T., who says this is a tradition resting on the authority of one Companion alone.'

[3] *Op. cit.*, pp. 172 ff.

This last is quoted by Tirmidhī, Nasāī, and Ibn Māja: 'Thou art my brother in this world and in the next.'

One of the clearest examples of hadith promulgated in the Alid interest is the following, taken from Ibn Māja: 'While we were with the prophet of God some young men of the Banū Hāshim approached. When the prophet saw them he shed tears and his countenance changed. I ('Abd Allah) said: "We see from your face that something troubles you," and he replied: "God has chosen for us, the ahlu-l-bait, the world to come rather than this world. After my time the people of my family will suffer misfortune: they will be dispersed and pursued until a people shall come from the East with black banners. They will ask for prosperity and will not obtain it. They will fight and will conquer and obtain what they asked. They will only receive it to render it to a man of my household. And he will fill the earth with justice just as they filled it with injustice.' A more obvious invention it would be difficult to discover. This hadith is one of the versions of the tradition known to Muhammadan savants as the 'hadith of the banners'. Of its author Ibn Ḥanbal remarks: 'His hadith are not hadith!' The first section, which apparently refers to the attempt made by Al Ma'mūn to secure the caliphate for the Alid, 'Alī b. Mūsā Al Riḍā,[1] has been added to the more widely received Mahdī tradition. In the Faḍāilu-l-Aṣḥāb it is recorded that the prophet gave the standard by which God was to give victory to his people into the hand of 'Alī, after curing him of a form of ophthalmia.

[1] *Al Fakhri*, ed. Cairo, 1317, p. 198.

It would seem that the theologians either would not or could not suppress traditions which had established themselves in the minds of the community and were generally recognized. They found it more convenient to promulgate other traditions which could not but tend to invalidate the claims the Shī'as rested on hadith admittedly in favour of 'Alī, as, for example, saying that Muhammad's infant son would have survived if it had been God's intention to send another prophet after him.[1] Again, the assertion of the Shī'as that the prophet had made a testamentary disposition in 'Alī's favour repeatedly finds mention in the canonical collections. Characteristically the aṣḥābu-l-ḥadīth leave those traditions obviously inspired by the 'Alids unaltered, and insert hadith which give them the lie direct. For example, 'Āisha is made to describe the last moments of her dying husband and exclaim: 'How could he have made any such disposition in these circumstances?'

Later, when the feeling between Shī'a and Sunnī became exacerbated, the former repudiated all traditions but their own, which they rested on the authority of 'Alī and his friends. This was naturally the only course open to them: they could not appeal to Ijmā', since they had never represented more than a fraction of the community, and the Sunnī traditions as a whole were useless for their purpose. The first written Alid collection was known as *Al Kāfī*, and was composed by Muhammad b. Ya'qūb Al Kulīnī, who died in 328. A great difference between the two great divisions of the Muhammadan world is in their Quranic exegesis.

[1] *Bukhārī*, Krehl, ii, p. 434.

The Alids accused Abū Bakr and 'Uthmān of having altered and suppressed words and verses in the Quran which exalted 'Alī, and the Shī'a collections of traditions explain what those words and verses are.[1] They abound in fanciful interpretations of obscure expressions, especially when 'Alī can be introduced in some eschatological role. The difference in Quranic exegesis was probably a fairly early stage in the controversy.

Unfortunately, in religious matters the Abbasids did not observe the broad-mindedness and tolerance their attitude to foreigners, including those who were obviously only nominal Muslims, would lead one to expect. With the admission of foreigners to the full privileges and brotherhood of Islam there came a greater insistence on uniformity within Islam. If, so far as concerns the Arab, racial consciousness was weakened, so far as concerned the Muhammadan religious consciousness was enormously strengthened. The proud and independent Arab, while his authority was undisputed, could afford to ignore for the most part the *dhimmis* who adhered to their religion ; but the Abbasid, who had thrown open the highes places in his kingdom to the foreigner, could not, or at any rate did not, accord the same toleration that Muhammad and his countrymen had displayed to the protected cults. With the Abbasid rule, the latent fanaticism of Islam burst forth, humiliating and subduing Jews and Christians to the position they occupy in purely Muhammadan countries to-day.

[1] See *Geschichte des Qorans*, Nöldeke-Schwally, Leipzig, 1919, pp. 93 ff.

It is not germane to our subject to inquire how far the caliphs themselves or their governors and generals obeyed in their private lives the injunctions of the prophet. The fact remains that the Abbasids officially supported the efforts of the doctors to restore the *sunna* of Muhammad throughout their vast dominions. Most of the Abbasids had a theological education from their tutors; and some one learned in religious matters was attached officially to the court. The religion of Islam became 'established'. Provincial governors were ordered to measure their actions by the standard of the Quran, and to uphold the authority of religious law. Now the pious could emerge from their obscurity and take their place in regulating the life of the individual and the community according to the laws which had been evolved and deduced during the century and more since the prophet's death. With the definitely religious bent of the administration their importance in the community was enormously enhanced. Now that the *sunna* was to be the norm of life it was discovered that the Muhammadan world did not know what the *sunna* was. It may easily be conjectured what was the depth of the ignorance in the distant provinces from Bukhārī's account of the conduct of public prayer in the mosque of Basra.[1] Before the task of 'reviving the *sunna*' could be begun it had first to be determined what was the practice of the prophet. Mālik in the middle of the second century could produce only six hundred sayings of the prophet of a legal character. Thus it is clear that the vast mass of material in the *sunna* was unknown to him.

[1] *v. s.*, p. 43.

The demand having arisen for a clear unequivocal ecclesiastical tradition, efforts were made by the religious and by the professional doctors to supply it. First there were those who applied the words of Muhammad, 'Seek knowledge even unto China,'[1] to the problem, believing that if they traversed the whole Muhammadan world and interrogated all who had been in converse with the Companions and Followers of the prophet, 'knowledge', the resultant body of traditional matter, would suffice to guide all Muslims in the right path.

Secondly there were those who frankly recognized that there was not a sufficient amount of tradition extant, nor in the nature of things could there ever have been, to provide guidance for the whole community in every department of private and public life in the changed circumstances of the time. These people claimed the right to frame laws by the exercise of reason and induction. Their school was known as the Aṣḥābu-l-Rai.

Thirdly there was the ignoble party, who shared neither the simple faith of the first nor the intellectual honesty of the second school. They claimed to be traditionists pure and simple and to base their findings on the traditions and customs of the prophet; but inasmuch as tradition was sometimes self-contradictory and sometimes non-existent they had to resort to a forced exegesis: the inductive method of the opponents they affected to despise; or to sheer invention.

The 'searchers after knowledge' (*Ṭālibūn al-'Ilm*) displayed a marvellous activity, some unquestioningly

[1] *Kanzu-l-'Ummāl*, v, p. 202.

undertaking the long and hazardous journey from the Guadalquiver to the Oxus in order to hear a hadith from the lips of one who claimed to have it in succession from Muhammad. In the second century a certain punctiliousness had to be observed. It was necessary to take over the hadith in its entirety, adding one's own name as the last link in the chain. It would be difficult to over-estimate the importance of this movement within Islam. Without the journeys and researches of these men the canonical collections would have been impossible. They kept alive in the memories of men scattered throughout the Muhammadan world a record of what the prophet was reported to have said and done. Nor was this all. They secured the general application of hadith which possessed only a local or provincial authority. In the nature of things, before the *sunna* was adopted by the government as an authoritative principle in the life of the state, no practice or doctrine—even if it were a genuine tradition of a Companion—could be guaranteed a hearing outside the circle of its original audience. But now that scholars travelled everywhere to supplement the traditions current in their own provinces and returned with their store to instruct an eager circle of pupils, the whole of the Muhammadan world had to listen to what was reported in its several districts. The summary report of Bukhārī's handling of the vast number of traditions current in his day (see p. 28 f.) is an indication of the general character of hadith in the third century. Some were deemed worthy of inclusion in the canonical corpus; the great majority had been coined to support doctrines current in particular areas.

Journeys in quest of knowledge were elevated into acts of consummate piety, so that, for example, he who died from perils by the way, or succumbed to privation, was likened to him who lost his life in fighting for the faith. The following, recorded by Al Tirmidhī, Ibn Māja, Ibn Ḥanbal, and Al Dārimī, illustrates the activity of the *Ṭālibu-l-ʿIlm*, and the esteem in which 'knowledge' was held by the pious Muslim: 'Kathīr b. Qais said: "I was sitting with Abū Dardā in the mosque of Damascus when a man came to him and said, 'I have come to you from Medina for a tradition which I have heard that you narrate from (*ʿan*) the apostle of God: for no other purpose have I come.'" ʿAbu Dardā said: "I heard the apostle of God say, 'Whoso travels a road in search of knowledge will God lead in a road to Paradise. Verily the angels joyfully spread their wings over the *Ṭālibu-l-ʿIlm*. All creatures in heaven and earth and even the fishes in the depth of the waters pray for the learned man (*alʿālim*). His superiority over the ordinary man is as that of the full moon over all the stars.'"' It would be difficult to find more fulsome praise of any human activity.

Both the strong religious motive and also the desire to pose before their countrymen as men who possessed traditions of prophetic origin which were not contained in written collections accounted for the longevity of the 'Quest for knowledge'.[1] Centuries after the canonical collections had become recognized as authoritative and binding on the conscience of the pious, Muslims still

[1] Al Suyūṭī (sub Mustʿaṣim) records that a number of traditionists granted this caliph a licence to repeat traditions in their name. This evidence from the seventh century of the Hijra is a striking example of the longevity of oral tradition.

undertook these journeys. The demand created the supply. There were not wanting charlatans who were willing to narrate any number of hadith for a sum of money. And as the *ṭālibūn* of later times were generally the most credulous of men, the wild stories which they brought back from their travels and related as sober traditions emanating from the founder of their religion ultimately brought the whole practice into contempt.

The very name of the second party—those who desired to frame the jurisprudence of the Islamic community by the aid of the vast amount of knowledge which had been acquired by its more enlightened members—is probably a reflection on their non-Arabian tenets. They were called the *Aṣḥābu-l-Rai*.[1] The early *fiqh* literature contains many axioms which are taken straight from Roman law-books. The foreign character of much of the *fiqh* was apparent to early Arabian writers, who do not hesitate to display their scorn for the methods of those who relied on members of a conquered race for the principles of their jurisprudential system rather than on the customs of the Arabs.

The third party to take a share in the work of providing the community with foundations for a rule of life and conduct were the Aṣḥābu-l-hadith. They were not, as we have seen, the first party in the field: probably they did not feel called upon to bestir themselves until they had amassed more traditional matter than was at their disposal when the Aṣḥābu-l-Ray first took the field. But the painstaking researches of the

[1] rai = *opinio*.

Ṭālibūn-al-ʿilm produced an ever-growing mass of hadith which could be drawn upon to support almost any doctrine or practice, so that they were able by supplementing this source from their own inventions to deny the necessity for the exercise of *opinio,* and to demand that the laws and customs of the community should be based on the *sunna* as it was embodied in the traditions of the prophet. It was this controversial necessity for the production of hadith which helped to swell the vast number of traditions ascribed to the prophet. But since custom and law had by this time become established in some respects both practically and theoretically, the controversy, like so many of the disputations of the Rabbis in the Talmud, was to a large extent robbed of practical value. It was a controversy to determine not so much what the law of the community should be, but rather on what principle it should rest—free and independent drawing from the legal systems of the civilized world, or the *sunna* of the prophet as reported by tradition.[1]

Despite the invention of hadith to support a principle required at the time, the existence of contradictory hadith, and the lack of any critical examination of the statements of the traditionists, the controversy ended in the complete victory of the traditional party, so that their doctrines have become an integral part of the faith of a Muhammadan.

[1] The comparison drawn between the corruption in law and custom introduced into Islam by the Shuʿūbiyya and the error into which Israel fell through the contamination of muwallidūn (*MS,* ii. 76, foot-note) is undoubtedly suggested by Jewish Haggada. Israel's apostasy and idolatry are constantly attributed to the presence of the 'mixed multitude' of Exodus xii. 38.

It must not be supposed that the representatives of these two opposing schools of thought were always divided into two sharply-divided camps.[1] Distinct as their methods were in principle, there were many of the most influential men in the world of Muslim jurisprudence who sought to confirm the findings of *rai* by the traditions of the orthodox, as did Al-Shaibānī. Moreover, on the other hand, *Al-Muwaṭṭa*, the law-book emanating from the 'home of the *sunna*', where hadith fails, appeals to *rai*.[2]

The attacks of the *Aṣḥābu-l-Rai* on the traditionists had a salutary effect; they were compelled to endeavour to put their house in order, and the beginnings of some sort of criticism of authorities may be traced. The flat contradiction existing between many of the hadith was obviously the favourite object of attack; and where such an accusation can be sustained there are only two replies. It must either be maintained that the contradiction is apparent rather than real,[3] or the inconvenient hadith must be thrown overboard.

[1] A protest against speculation and the enmity subsisting between the schools is preserved by Bukhārī (Krehl, p. 282, Bābu Ta'līmi-l-Farāiḍ: 'Beware of conjecture (*ẓann*), for conjecture is the most lying hadith. Do not scrutinize everything exhaustively nor dwell in hatred and mutual dislike, but be servants of God as brethren.' These, says Abū Huraira, were the prophet's words.

[2] See, further, D. B. Macdonald, *Muslim Theology*, London, 1903, pp. 100 ff.

[3] Any collection of hadith which is provided with a commentary will show the straits to which harmonists are reduced. Cf. e.g. *Mishkāt*, p. 351, sub *intaqasa*, note 5. Almost every page is occupied with a discussion of this kind. 'There are few chapters of Muhammadan jurisprudence in which the underlying traditions are free from contradictions': Goldziher.

Already Al-Shāfiʿī (d. 204) lays down principles by which contradictory hadith can be made to explain and complement each other, while Ibn Qutaiba displays great ingenuity in this field, as the following examples from the *Mukhtalifu-l-ḥadīth* [1] will show:

'The ahlu-l-kalām assert that the two following hadith are contradictory and mutually exclusive, namely:

(*a*) There will be no prophet after me, and no religion after my religion. The lawful and the unlawful will be what God has permitted and forbidden according to my words until the last day.

(*b*) The Messiah will descend and slay swine, break the cross, and add to the lawful. And from ʿĀisha: Say of the Apostle of God, "The seal of the prophets": do not say, "There will be no prophet after him."'

Now we maintain that there is no contradiction whatever in these statements; for the Messiah was an earlier prophet whom God took up (to Himself) and will send him down again at the end of the age as a sign (*ʿalaman*) of the Hour. As God has said: 'Verily he shall be a sign (*ʿilmun*) of the hour. Doubt not then of it'; [2] and some Readers read 'as a sign' (*ʿalamun*). And when the Messiah descends he will not abrogate anything that Muhammad the apostle of God commanded, nor will the Imām from his religion [3] be first, but he will set him (Muhammad) first and pray behind him. As to the words 'and add to the lawful', a man said to Abū Huraira, 'He will only add women to the lawful,' to which he answered with

[1] Cairo, 1326 A.H., pp. 235–6.

[2] Sur. 43, v. 61, lit. 'He is for knowledge of the Hour'.

[3] Or, 'people'.

a laugh, 'Precisely.' The words 'and add to the lawful' do not mean that he will allow men to marry five or six wives: they merely mean that whereas when the Messiah was first on earth he did not marry, when God sends him down again he will marry a woman and will add to what God has made lawful to him, i.e. the addition is from God. Then will there be no Christians but will know that he is the servant of God and be certain that he is mortal.

As to 'Āisha's words, they refer to the descent of Jesus and consequently do not contradict the prophet's saying: 'There will be no prophet after me.' He meant there will be no prophet after me to abrogate my commands as is customarily the prophet's mission. Her meaning was, 'Do not say that the Messiah will not come down after him.'

The contradictory import of traditions authorizing or prohibiting the writing of traditions has been referred to above (p. 16). Our author[1] deals with them thus:

(*a*) Do not write anything from me except the Quran. Whoso writes anything from me, destroy him.

(*b*) From 'Abd Allah b. 'Amr. I said to the apostle of God shall I record knowledge (*'ilm*). Yes, said he. From Shu'aib: May I write down all that I hear from thee of the things that please (God) or displease Him? Yes, said the apostle, for I speak nothing but the truth.

Here, say the philosophers, is a blatant inconsistency. Now we say that there are two meanings to these hadith. One, that a *sunna* is abrogated by a *sunna*, for he at first forbade that his words should be written down; then afterwards when he knew that *sunnas* would be multiplied and escape the memory he

[1] p. 365.

agreed to their being recorded in writing. Two, the permission was peculiar to 'Abd Allah b. 'Amr because he read the books of the earlier monotheists and used to write in Syriac and Arabic, while the rest of the Companions were illiterate (*ummiyīn*), only one or two of them being able to write, and they not correctly. Therefore, because the prophet feared that they would write inaccurately he forbade them to write anything, and because he could trust 'Abd Allah b. 'Amr's ability he allowed him to record his saying (pp. 365–6).

Again the question, May a Muslim drink standing?

(*a*) Anas says the prophet forbade it.

(*b*) Ibn 'Umar says the prophet used to drink standing.

There is no contradiction, says Ibn Qutaiba, because the prophet forbade drinking while one is walking. He wanted people to eat and drink in comfort, and not to drink while hurrying on a journey or business. Neglect of this precaution causes choking and indigestion; moreover, the word *qum* implies walking, not mere standing. (Here follows a quotation from Al 'Asha where *yaqūmu 'alā* means 'proceed against'.) In the second hadith 'drinking while standing', *qāimun*, not walking nor active is meant. There is nothing objectionable in that because he was at his ease, which is after all as though he were seated (*bi-manzilati-l-qā 'id*).

To a modern reader these explanations will seem more ingenious than convincing.[1]

Despite the power which a well-disposed government

[1] An interesting discussion of the contradictory traditions as to the age of the prophet at his death will be found in Al Mas'ūdī, *Les Prairies d'Or*, Paris, 1914, Tome iv, pp. 148 ff.

gave to the traditionists they could not dominate the everyday life of the Muhammadan entirely by their theories. And often custom and practice were not in agreement with the *sunna* and hadith. When these differences were merely local something could perhaps be done by an ecclesiastically-minded governor who was not unwilling to apply the civil power to bring about conformity. But when the differences were in customs which had become almost universal the traditionist had to yield. Two lines of retreat were open to him. Either he must declare that the ḥadīth was invalid and had been abrogated by another (a device familiar to the Quran exegetes),[1] or he must admit that universal practice was invested with a higher power than ḥadīth. This would seem to be a jeopardous step, but the traditionists were fully equal to the occasion. They elevated the agreed practice of the community to the position of an authoritative principle—*al Ijmāʿ*—and asserted that when *ijmāʿ* was in contradiction with the *sunna* it was a clear indication that an abrogating hadith had been lost! Ibn Qutaiba, however, does not feel himself called upon to go to such lengths to justify the hadith. He asserts roundly that *ijmāʿ* is a more trustworthy guide than ḥadīth; for the latter is subject to change through the carelessness of the narrators, to obscurity, abrogation, and forgery, while *ijmāʿ* is not liable to such mishaps: hence the cause of the conflict between tradition and practice.

But the doctrine which satisfactorily set aside all disquieting reflections on the possibility of untrust-

[1] Ibn ʿUmar in Al Dāraquṭnī (*Mishkāt*, p. 24), explicitly: *inna aḥādīthanā yunsakhu baʿḍuhā baʿḍan kanaskhi-l-qurāni.*

worthy traditions was enshrined in the words, 'My people will never agree upon an error.' This tradition is not to be found in the *Ṣaḥīḥān*, though it is recorded by Abū Dāūd and Al-Tirmidhī as *ḥasan*. The promulgation of this doctrine was truly masterly. We cannot but admire the resource and ingenuity of those who, threatened with the destruction—or at all events the discrediting—of their elaborate structure of tradition, incorporated the destructive force in their system and invested it with the authority of the prophet himself.[1]

[1] It is obvious that this doctrine of the infallibility of the community as a whole provides an open road for the free development of the Muhammadan peoples. Any intelligent student of contemporary literature can see that the leaders of Muhammadan thought, when popular feeling is behind them, have no difficulty in obtaining the support of a large section of the Islamic world in favour of men and causes that would be condemned by orthodox tradition—the caliphate question is an interesting example. The words of a great scholar and man of affairs, written forty years ago (*Annals of the Early Caliphate*, by Sir W. Muir, London, 1883, p. 456, as quoted by Cheragh Ali), are hardly true of the Muhammadan world to-day: 'Islam is stationary; swathed in the rigid bands of the Coran; it is powerless, like the Christian dispensation, to adapt itself to the varying circumstances of time and place, and to keep pace with, if not to lead and direct, the progress of society and the elevation of the race. In the body politic the spiritual and the secular are hopelessly confounded, and we fail of perceiving any approach to free institutions or any germ whatever of popular government.' The Muhammadanism of the present day differs from the letter of its ancient documents in many important particulars, and given the impetus from within there is great scope for reform and development.

IV

CRITICISM OF HADITH BY MUSLIMS

Minatory hadith against liars in tradition; the 'quṣṣāṣ'.—Hadith as a study.—Method of Muslim criticism.—The categories of hadith.—Ibn Khaldun's verdict on tradition.—Modern criticism by Muslims.

We have examined some of the influences which were at work during the formative period of Islam, and seen how they have all left their mark on tradition. It now remains to review briefly the criticism of hadith by Muhammadans themselves. It is quite impossible here to attempt to give a *résumé* of the opinions formed by the principal Arabic writers. In general, perhaps, it may be said that, like most Oriental authors, without feeling themselves in any way bound to take into account the trustworthiness of their sources, they used the hadith literature as a quarry from which to extract whatever they considered relevant to their purpose. Some writers who were not afraid to subject the canonical literature to some sort of criticism will be noticed.

The two judgements which Muhammadans themselves have passed on hadith have been admirably summarized by Dr. Nicholson:[1] 'While every impartial student will admit the justice of Ibn Qutayba's claim that no religion has such historical attestations as Islam—*laysa li-ummatin mina 'l-umami asnādun ka-asnādihim*—he must at the same time cordially assent to the observation made by another Muhammadan:

[1] *A Literary History of the Arabs*, London, 1907, p. 145.

"In nothing do we see pious men more given to falsehood than in Tradition" (*lam nara 'l-ṣāliḥīna fī shayin akdhaba minhum fi 'l-ḥadīth*).' The latter statement was made by 'Āsim al-nabīl (d. 212): almost the same words are reported to have been said by Yahyā b. Sa'īd (d. 192); both of them were active nearly a century before the compilation of the first corpus of canonical tradition. Al-Zuhrī is reported to have said that the reason he wrote down hadith was because of the prevalence of traditions emanating from the East whose authenticity he denied.[1]

A most significant recognition within hadith itself of the untrustworthiness of guarantors is to be found in Bukhārī.[2] Ibn 'Umar reports that Muhammad ordered all dogs to be killed save sheep-dogs and hounds. Abū Huraira added the word *au zar'in*; whereupon Ibn 'Umar makes the remark, 'Abū Huraira owned cultivated land!'[3] A better illustration of the underlying motive of some hadith can hardly be found.

Weighty pronouncements against what was becoming a universal evil produced a reaction. Men came to see that the union of truth and falsehood might result in the complete overthrow of apostolic tradition. A most remarkable feature of the reaction was that the theologians borrowed the weapons of the liars. In order to combat false traditions they invented others equally destitute of prophetic authority. An extraordinary number of Companions are cited as witnesses

[1] *JASB*, 1856, p. 322.

[2] *Kitābu-l-Ṣaid*, Bab. 6.

[3] Cf. Tirmidhi, i, p. 281, and *MS*, ii, p. 49 and the notes there (to which add Ibn Māja, Bāb Qatli-l-kilābi, illa kalb ṣaidin au zar'in). I do not find Ibn 'Umar's damaging observation on Abū Huraira in Krehl or Houdas *in loc.*

that the prophet said, 'Whoever shall repeat of me that which I have not said, his resting-place shall be in hell.'[1] A study of the theological systems of the world would hardly reveal a more naïve attempt to tread the *ṣirāṭu-l-mustaqīm*! Other pseudo-prophetic hadith portray Muhammad warning his people against liars who will seek to mislead the community while claiming his authority for so doing.

However, the threat of eternal damnation was not thought to be sufficient in itself to secure the community against the forgeries of the unscrupulous. The matter soon, moreover, became one of political urgency. Such chapters as we now find in the canonical traditions dealing with the merits of the heroes of the different factions of Islam had a profound influence on the popular mind. Obviously much might be done by promulgating the *Faḍāil 'Alī*,[2] or, on the other hand, the *Faḍāil 'Uthmān*, in a province which had heard of neither. In fact, according to the express statement of Muslim, criticism of hadith owed its rise to the great dynastic struggles of the second century, when the empire was split into hostile camps, each of them supporting their pretensions by a claim to apostolic authority. Criticism of hadith was keenest in those regions where political and religious differences were most felt, notably in the Iraq. As we have seen, it centred not on the subject-matter but on the chain of guarantors, though perhaps, since Orientals are the best judges of Oriental mentality, the result was very

[1] Cf. Muir, *LM*, 1912, p. xxxvi. The saying is to be found in all collections.

[2] The hadith extolling his merits and establishing his claim to the highest place in the prophet's estimation.

much the same. Hadith was not criticized from the point of view of what was inherently reasonable and to be regarded as worthy of credence,[1] but from a consideration of the reputation which the guarantors of the tradition bore. However, the doctrine of Ijmāʿ may have had a restraining influence on purely subjective criticism, for quite early it had been extended to cover the sphere of hadith, and what the community agreed upon was above serious questioning.

However, there was still a large circle outside the orthodox thinkers who rejected the whole system of hadith. They were not concerned to adopt those which happened to fit in with the views and doctrines of the doctors, or even with those which might fairly be held to support their own view of life. So far from being impressed by the earnestness of the traditionists who scrupulously examined the *isnād*, or by the halo of sanctity which had gathered round the early guarantors of tradition, the independent thinkers of the second and third centuries openly mocked and derided the system as a whole and the persons and matters named therein. Some of the most flagrant examples of these lampoons will be found in the *Book of Songs*, where indecent stories are cast into the form in which tradition was customarily handed down to posterity.

Nor were these careless free-lances alone in attacking the elaborate system which was being built up on the foundation of the supposed utterances of the prophet. Popular as such literature was among *savants* and

[1] I except, of course, the great philosophical historian Ibn Khaldūn, who expressly says, 'the rule for distinguishing what is true from what is false in history is based on its possibility or impossibility,' quoted by Nicholson, *LHA*, p. 438.

vulgar alike, a more serious enemy to the orthodox entered the field. The many mutually contradictory traditions coined to establish dogmatic and legal points were intolerable to contemporary philosophers, who eagerly seized upon hadith which had been discredited by the conscience of Islam. The presence of folk-lore and fable whose heathen origin was well known to the learned could not but excite contempt, and the hadith which were borrowed direct from Jewish Haggāda and Christian legend were especially vulnerable to attack. Their presence is deprecated by speeches attributed to the prophet in other hadith, and Ibn Qutaiba boldly throws them overboard. As Ibn Khaldūn says, the Arabs were an ignorant race, with no literary nor scientific knowledge, and when they wished to probe the mysteries of creation and the universe they turned for information to the Jews who had accepted Islam. These, says this learned author, were no less ignorant than the surrounding Arabs; but they brought over into Islam a mass of their own traditions, especially those dealing with the origin of the creation and with the future of the human race. Commentaries were soon filled with their stories. So great was their reputation with the Muslims that their fables and pseudo-prophetic hadith were accepted despite the fact that all proof of the speakers' veracity or the intrinsic probability of the stories were lacking. These Jews included natives of the Yaman such as Ka'bu-l Aḥbar (d. 32) and Wahb b. Munabbih (d. 114) and 'Abd Allah b. Salam (d. 43).

The popularity of these moralizing stories, whatever their source, among the Ascetics and Moralists, and also among the general public, has ensured them a permanent place in Muslim tradition. Despite their vulnerable *isnāds*, the later collectors accepted them for the sake of their valuable influence in the sphere of morals and ethics. Nemesis followed hard on this weakness, for, as we have seen, the fables were on the one hand a cause of embarrassment in dealing with the attacks of the learned; and the public on the other hand showed a marked preference for the lying and impudent inventions of the street story-tellers, the *quṣṣāṣ*, who clothed their nonsense in the garb of a canonical *sanad.*[1] Unless the ears of the simple believer had been tickled and his curiosity stimulated by these haggadic stories the *quṣṣāṣ* could never have entered into competition with the *muḥaddithūn.* So great was the effrontery of these street orators and fablemongers that the saintly Ibn Ḥanbal had to flee before them.

[1] The following two illustrations of the methods of these plausible rascals deserve mention, as they are not without humour, and show how incredibly credulous the ordinary ignorant Muslim was:

(*a*) 'The poet Kulthūm b. ʿAmr al ʿAttābī, who lived in the time of Hārūn and Al-Maʾmūn, collected a crowd round him in a mosque of the capital, and gave out the following hadith in the correct form: "He who can touch the end of his nose with the tip of his tongue can be certain that he will never feel the flames of hell." As though a signal had been given the whole company put out their tongues to see whether they had the visible mark of those destined for Paradise.' *MS*, ii, p. 164.

(*b*) 'They collect a great crowd of people round them: one Qāṣṣ stations himself at one end of the street and narrates traditions about the merits of ʿAlī, while his fellow stands at the other end of the street exalting the virtues of Abū Bakr. Thus they secure the pence of the Nāṣibī as well as the Shīʿi, and divide their gains equally afterwards.' *Ib.*, pp. 165 f.

But in matters of jurisprudence the traditionists refused to yield. On the contrary, one result of the attack on tradition was to enhance its authority, as the following hadith, which are now canonical, will demonstrate: 'Verily I have brought the Quran and along with it that which is similar thereto, yet the rich man on his throne would say, "Hold fast the Quran and its injunctions to enjoy and to refrain." But verily what the apostle of God has declared unlawful God has made unlawful. . . .' Again: 'Does any one of you suppose that God has not forbidden anything but what is contained in this Quran? Verily by God that which I have commanded, admonished, and forbidden is like unto the Quran and more than it. And God does not permit you to enter the houses of the People of the Book without their permission, nor to beat their wives and eat their fruit, provided they have paid their taxes.' Nothing could be more explicit than this assertion of the authority of the oral law enshrined in tradition.

But this position involved the giving of some sort of guarantee that traditions were authentic, and so, when in the third century the compilation of the canonical collections was begun, a systematic selection of trustworthy traditions—trustworthy, that is, in the uncritical estimation of the collectors—became an integral part of the science of tradition. Inquiries were made as to the character of the guarantors, whether they were morally and religiously satisfactory, whether they were tainted with heretical doctrines, whether they had a reputation for truthfulness, and had the ability to transmit what they had themselves heard. Finally, it was necessary that they should be competent witnesses whose testimony would be accepted in a court of civil law.[1]

In Muslim's day the great importance of hadith, as a study in itself, was clearly recognized, for we find in his collection[2] the saying: 'Verily this science[3] is a religion: take care on whose authority you receive your religion.' There are also the solemn words: 'The *isnād* is a matter of religion; and were it not for the *isnād* any one could say what he pleased' (*laula-l-isnādu laqāla man shā'a mā shā'a*): in other words, the *isnād* was regarded as a protection against forgery and invention, as it well may have been with the religiously-minded Muslims. Muslim himself evidently does not feel comfortable about the selection he has made from the content of Muhammadan tradition. He tells us on the authority of Ibn Sīrīn that 'people used not to ask questions about the *isnād*, but when dissension (*fitna*)[4] broke out they said, "Tell us the names of your authorities." So the *ahlu-l-ṣunna* were scrutinized and their hadith received, and the *ahlu-l-bida'* were scrutinized

[1] *JASB*, 1856, p. 53. [2] *Bāb Al Isnād min al Dīn.*

[3] The 'Science of Tradition' determines what is to be understood by a saying or action of the prophet which forms the subject of tradition. It is defined in the *Dictionary of Technical Terms* . . ., ed. A. Sprenger, Calcutta, 1862, p. 27, thus: 'The science of tradition is that science by which the sayings and doings of the prophet of God are known. As to his sayings, they are in the Arabic tongue, and consequently he who is unacquainted with Arabic is unable to acquire this science. It may be something said by itself or in a context, metaphorical or literal, general or particular, absolute or qualified, explicit or implicit, and so on, according to the rules of Arabic. . . . As to his doings, they are the things which he did of himself, whether he commanded us to follow him therein or not, as for example, actions which he did naturally or out of some individual characteristic.'

[4] On the double meaning of this word see Bukhārī, *Kitābu-l-Ṣaum.*

nd their hadith were not received.' In the same hapter he mentions that traditions—which the context suggests were in some way suspicious—were received as genuine because the people who reported them were notoriously pious Muslims.

He adds the exceedingly important note that in his day the traditionists (*ahlul 'Ilm*) frequently suspected reporters of tradition, but that they did not feel it incumbent upon them to expose their faults and to give a decision against them, except where serious interests were involved. He strongly deprecates this carelessness on the ground that false hadith constitute a standing menace to Islam. He urges that the utmost pains should be taken to brand such traditions false and unworthy of credence, and he has only contempt for those who, knowing that traditions are weak, wilfully repeat them in order to be accounted learned and pious. 'He that thus treads the path of knowledge has no part in it, and ought to be called ignorant rather than learned,' says Muslim.

The three categories into which all traditions were divided were sound (*ṣaḥīḥ*), fair (*ḥasan*), and weak (*ḍa'īf*). One of the great differences between the collections of Bukhārī and Muslim[1] was that the former refused to regard hadith *mu'an'an* as standing in the same category as those which contained words like 'I heard' or 'I saw' the Prophet of God, or 'So-and-so informed me'. Unless some word implying personal contact between two guarantors was used in a tradition Bukhārī maintained that Islam could not apply it to establish any law. To him and to rigorists in tradition

[1] *Supra*, p. 32.

all other traditions were at the best a sort of apocrypha. It rather looks as if Muslim, when he attacks an anonymous contemporary (*ba 'ḍu 'l-muntaḥali 'l-ḥadīth min ahli 'asrinā*) and asserts that the expression *'an* implies personal contact unless there is direct evidence to the contrary, has Bukhārī in mind. He accuses his opponent of inconsistency on the ground that there are several hadith *mu'an'an* which are accepted as genuine, e.g. Hishām *'an abīhi*. In this and similar cases, he argues, it would be ridiculous to suppose that there was no personal contact between the two men, and to refuse to regard the tradition as genuine.

The classification of traditions is a highly technical pursuit, and a new terminology had to be evolved to indicate the numerous kinds of tradition current in the Muhammadan world.

The Muslim doctors' view of tradition, as given by Al Jurjānī (d. 816), is both detailed and clear, and is substantially the same as that which has always prevailed among his co-religionists. He says with good reason that the text of a tradition is rarely taken into account, and that criticism is confined to the *isnād*. He accepts the three categories given above, and defines and subdivides them at length thus:

1. *Ṣaḥīḥ* or sound tradition.

musnad. A tradition which is supported by authorities resting on the prophet.

muttaṣal. With a continuous uninterrupted *isnād*. If it does not go back to the prophet it is said to be *mauqūf* stopped.

marfū'. Carried back and attributed to the prophet; i.e. it may be *muttaṣal* or *mauqūf*.

mu'an'an. Linked by the word 'from' instead of a word implying personal contact.

mu'allaq. Suspended with the name of a guarantor or more missing. If the name is missing from the middle it is *munqata'*; if from the end it is *mursal* (*v.i.*).

fard. Unique; peculiar to one district. Sometimes it means peculiar to one reporter, in which case it may be weak.

mudraj. One which has been glossed or interpolated by one of the first reporters.

mashhūr. Well known, and from many reporters.

gharīb. Resting on the authority of only one person.

'azīz. Resting on the authority of two or three persons.

muṣaḥḥaf. Badly written either in respect to the name of a guarantor or with a variant reading in the *matn.*

musalsal. With a chain going back to the prophet containing the formula 'I heard' and so on.

2. *Da'īf* or weak.

mauqūf. Stopped short of the prophet, and therefore no legal proof.

maqtū'. Cut off. Emanating from the 'Followers' as to their sayings and doings. Not a legal proof.

mursal. A saying of the Followers that the prophet did or said so-and-so.

munqata'. Severed, i.e. a link is missing.

mu'ḍal. One or more names missing, e.g. a statement of Mālik that Muhammad said.

shādh. At variance with another well-tested tradition.

munkar. A weak tradition at variance with another weak one.

mu'allal. With a hidden fault or inconsistency.

mudallas. With a hidden fault: either personal intercourse is falsely claimed between guarantors, or the name of one has been intentionally disguised by means of an appellative.

muḍṭarab. Deranged by verbal inconsistencies with another tradition.

maqlūb. One known to have come from a person other than the one named.

mauḍū'. Supposititious; hearsay which may be truth or mere invention.

3. *Ḥasan* or fair tradition is that which stands midway between genuine and weak. It may be either genuine or false. It is fair because nothing is known against the character of its reporter, and because it can sometimes be supported by other evidence.

The reader will probably agree with Al Jurjānī's saying that 'further examination into the distinction of names, titles, epithets, and degrees appertaining to the science would be a lengthy matter', and be content with a perusal of these and the other technical terms given in the appendix.[1] As an example of the application of this systematic criticism the following extracts from Abū Dāūd may be of interest:[2]

'Dies ist ein verwerfliches (*munkar*) Hadith, niemand anders hat es überliefert als Yazīd al Dālānī von Qatāda . . . Abū Dāwūd sagt: Ich habe das Hadith des Yazīd al Dālānī dem Aḥmad b. Ḥanbal vorgelegt, er hat mich aber hart zurückgewiesen, weil er es als krasse Fälschung betrachtete, er sagte: Was hat Jazīd . . . unter den Genossen des Qatāda zu suchen, hat er sich ja nicht um Hadith gekümmert! . . .

'Dieses Hadith ist nicht stark (*qawī*), Muslim b. Khālid ist schwach (*da'īf*). . . Ein schwacher Gewährs-

[1] Much information is to be found in the *Dictionary of Technical Terms used in the Sciences of the Musalmans*, ed. A. Sprenger, Calcutta, *sub* The Science of Tradition, and in his article in *ZDMG*, x, 1856, pp. 1–15, *Über das Traditionswesen bei den Arabern*. See also Edward E. Salisbury, *Contributions from Original Sources to our Knowledge of the Science of Muslim Tradition*, in *JAOS*, vii, 1862, pp. 60–142, to whom I owe the foregoing.

[2] Abū Dāūd, Cairo, 1280, i, p. 20, quoted in *MS*, ii, p. 251.

mann, beide Hadithe sind falsch (*wahm*) . . . nach einem Isnad: Al Ḥajjāj 'an Al Zuhrī. Dies ist ein schwaches Hadith, Al Ḥajjāj hat den Zuhrī nie gesehen und nie von ihm gehört, auch Ja'far b. Rabī'a hat den Zuhrī nie gesehen, dieser hat nur schriftlich mit jenem verkehrt.' (p. 197.)

The importance and value of the examination of the *isnād* is obvious. By impugning the bona fides of a guarantor—the process was called *jarḥ* or *ṭa'an*, i.e. wounding the reputation—thousands of untrustworthy traditions were eliminated from the canonical collections. On the other hand, if the subject-matter (*matn*) contained an obvious absurdity or an anachronism there was no ground for rejecting the hadith if the *isnād* was sound. This is the reason why there are so many hadith of a contradictory import in one and the same *bāb*. Historical difficulties within the *matn* could not arise when once the prophetic power of Muhammad was established as an article of faith. The existence to this day of such hadith as those quoted in Chapters V and VI can only be accounted for when the amazing credulity of the Muhammadan community is realized.

It is refreshing, after perusing these, to read the sane remarks of Ibn Khaldun[1] on a subject which more than once within living memory has profoundly stirred a Muhammadan country.

'The whole body of Muslims throughout the centuries have held that at the end of the age a man of the family of the prophet must appear who will strengthen religion and make justice manifest. The Muslims will follow him, and he will gain possession of the Muslim kingdoms, and be called Al Madhī.

[1] *Al Muqaddima*, Beyrut, ch. 52, p. 271.

Al-Dajjāl (the Antichrist) will come and afterwards the signs of the (last) hour indicated in the Ṣaḥīḥ. Then Jesus will descend from heaven and kill Al-Dajjāl; or, as some say, will descend with him (Al Mahdi) and help him to kill Al-Dajjāl, and will have the Mahdi as Imām in prayer. On this subject ḥadīth are cited as proof which the Imāms have published, though there are not wanting those who deny their authenticity, often comparing them with other reports. . . . We will now quote the ḥadīth that bear on this matter; the objections which have been made to them; and the ground on which the objections rest. . . . We say, then, that many of the Imāms have published ḥadīth about the Mahdī, namely, Al Tirmidhī, Abū Dāūd, Al Bazzār, Ibn Māja, Al Hākim, Ṭabarānī, and Abu Ya'la al-Mausilī. They carry back the traditions to many of the companions like 'Alī, Ibn 'Abbās, Ibn Umar, Ṭalḥa, Ibn Mas'ūd, Abu Huraīra, Anas, Abū Sa'īd al-Khudrī, Um Habība, Thaubān, Qurra ibn Aias, 'Alī al Hilālī, and 'Abd Allah b. al Ḥārith b. Juzī. The genuineness of the isnāds has often been denied, as we shall explain; but, as the doctors of hadith know, impugning (*jarḥ*) precedes justification (*ta'dīl*). If we find any of the guarantors of tradition convicted (*ṭa'an*) of carelessness, defective memory, weakness, or lack of judgement, the soundness of the ḥadīth is thereby adversely affected and its value decreased. If it be argued that on these grounds guarantors accepted by the authors of the Ṣaḥiḥān are affected (we may reply) that Ijmā' has agreed to accept the works of these two writers, and public conduct ('aml) is based on their contents. Ijmā' is the greatest protection and the best defence. No other work can be put in the same sure category (as the Ṣaḥiḥān). Nevertheless we find ground for discussion as to their isnāds in what has been handed down by doctors of ḥadīth.'

Our author then proceeds to quote a long extract from the work of Al-Suhailī (d. 581) on the authority of Abū Bakr b. Abū Khaithama (d. 279), of which we give a summary. 'He (apparently Abu Bakr)[1] says: the following hadith rests on the authority of only one companion and comes from al Iskāf:

1. The prophet of God said: "He who disbelieves in the Mahdī is an infidel, and he who disbelieves in Al Dajjāl is an infidel."' Now he says the same thing of the sun rising in the west—sufficient indication of exaggeration! Moreover, God knows whether he is right in carrying back the tradition to Mālik. At any rate, Al Iskāf with the doctors is suspect and an inventor.

2. (*a*) Tirmidhī and Abū Dāūd publish a tradition resting on the authority of Ibn 'Abbās[2] by way of 'Āṣim (d. 127), one of the seven readers, Zirr b. Ḥubaish and 'Abd Allah b. Mas'ūd from the prophet. 'Though the world had but a day to exist God would prolong that day until he sent a man of mine or of my family whose name is my name and whose father's name is as my father's name.' So Abū Dāūd without comment. Now he says in his celebrated epistle that what is cited in his book without comment is true.

(*b*) Tirmidhī's version is: 'The world shall not pass away until a man of my family and of my name shall reign over the Arabs.' And elsewhere with the variant 'until a man of my family shall be in power' (*wala*). Both of them are *ḥasan ṣaḥīḥ*. Moreover,

[1] One cannot always determine the author of certain passages. None of the writers systematically documents his sources, and therefore the comments may emanate from our author or his primary or secondary authority.

[2] Either this is a mistake for Ibn Mas'ūd, as I suspect (Ibn Abbas and Ibn Mas'ūd were both named 'Abd 'Allah); or, since they were contemporaries, the tradition was attributed to them both.

he relates them *mauqūf* on the authority of Abū Huraira. Al Ḥākim says that Al Thaurī (d. 161), Shu'ba (d. 160), Zāida, and other Imāms of the Muslims relate the same from 'Āṣim.

The following summary of the judgements passed on the said 'Āṣim as a traditionist is most instructive:

Al Ḥākim. Ṣaḥīḥ. 'Āsim was a Muslim Imām.

Aḥmad b. Ḥanbal (d. 241). An honest, trustworthy man; but Al-A'amash (d. 148) had a better memory; and Shu'ba, too, preferred him to 'Āsim. Al-'Ajli (d. 261) did not accept his authorities (Zirr and Abū Wāil) (d. 79), and regarded traditions from these men as weak.

Muhammad b. Sa'd (d. 230). Truthful, though he made many mistakes in hadith.

Ya'qūb b. Sufyān (d. 288). Confused (*mudṭarab*).

'Abd al Rahmān b. Abī Ḥātim (d. 327). 'I said to my father "Abu Zara' says that 'Āṣim is trustworthy." He replied he is not.'

Ibn 'Ulayya (d. 193). All the 'Āṣims have bad memories.

Abū Ḥātim (d. 275). Trustworthy and honest in ḥadīth, but he has not a retentive memory. Al Nasāī's judgement on him is not consistent.

Ibn Hirash (? Khirash d. 322). Disapproves of his hadith.

Abū Ja'far al 'Aqalī (d. 322). He had nothing but a bad memory.

Al Dāraqutnī (d. 385). Has somewhat to say about his memory.

Yaḥyā b. Al Qaṭṭān (d. 198). Every 'Āsim I have ever met had a bad memory. I heard Shu'ba say "'Āsim b. Abū Nujūd told me traditions, but I kept my own opinion about them.'[1]

Al Dhahabī. As a Qurān reader he was trustworthy,

[1] Read *fī nafsī* for *fil-nāsi.*

but not as a traditionist, though by nature truthful. His traditions are *ḥasan*.

Ibn Khaldūn remarks that if it be objected that the two shaikhs have published traditions from 'Āsim, it may be replied that they have only done so when his reports have been confirmed by others; not solely on his authority. But God knows best.

The reader would only be wearied by further examples of Ibn Khaldūn's exhaustive investigation of the authority for the belief in the coming of the Mahdī. But it is interesting to notice that he makes the point that there is no mention whatever of the Mahdī in Muslim's Ṣaḥīḥ; and that of the relevant traditions elsewhere only a few are free from taint. Moreover, a tradition which can claim some measure of support credits the Prophet with the utterance, 'There is no Mahdī except Jesus the son of Mary.'[1]

The extraordinary reverence in which the Ṣaḥīḥ of Bukhārī was held naturally deterred Muslim scholars from criticizing its contents. Within a century of its appearance it was hailed by a writer as the prophet's own book, and the prestige of the work grew with the advancing years. Bukhārī was regarded as a saint, and pilgrimages were made to his tomb: the possession even of a copy of his book was held to be a sure protection against disaster.

Although such an exalted position was not attained

[1] The Isnād given is: Muḥammad b. Khālid Al Jundī from Abbān b. Sālih b. Abī 'Ayyāsh from Al Ḥasan al Baṣrī from Anas b. Mālik. The judgements on these are as follows: Yahya b. Ma'īn says Muh. ibn Khālid is trustworthy. Al Baihaqī, it is unique. Al Ḥākim says the isnad occurs in different forms, *mursal*. Abu 'Ayyāsh is branded as *matrūk* by Baihaqī; it is *munqaṭa'*; in short, the tradition is *ḍa'īf* and *muḍṭarab*.

by Muslim and his work, yet it has always been bracketed with the Ṣaḥīḥ of Bukhārī, and they are cited as The Two Ṣaḥīḥs (Ṣaḥīḥān). But inasmuch as the ground of the authority of the Ṣaḥīḥān was their acceptance by the general consent of the Islamic community, and they had not been subjected to any systematic critical examination, some dissentient voices have been raised against them from the earliest times down to the present day. Like the customs they sought to authorize by appeal to apostolic custom and precept, they owe their position to *ijma'*, not to their inherent virtue and faultlessness. Al Dāraquṭnī (d. 385) devotes a book (*al Istidrakat wal Tatabbu'*) to the demonstration of the weakness of many of the canonical traditions, while Abū Dāūd and his disciples claim for his work a higher position than that of any collection of hadith. Again, Ibn 'Abd al Barr (d. 463) and Al Nawawī (d. 676) do not hesitate to assail traditions which seem to them to be contrary to reason or derogatory to the dignity of the prophet. However, though theologians down to the ninth century inveighed against particular hadith in the canonical collections, the authority of the Ṣaḥīḥān as the content of genuine apostolic tradition as a whole was not called in question.

Modern Criticism of Tradition by Muslims.

The study of hadith and hadith-criticism in Muslim academies still continues on the lines laid down a thousand years ago; and it is interesting to see how the modern educated Muslim regards this activity.

The extracts that follow are taken from 'A critical exposition of the popular "Jihad" . . . by Moulavi Cheragh Ali.'[1]

'The biographers of Mohammad and the narrators of his campaigns are too lax in enumerating the expeditions led by Mohammad. They have noted down the names and accounts of various expeditions without having due regard to a rational criticism, or without being bound by the stringent laws of the technical requirements of traditionary evidence. Consequently they give us romances of the expeditions without specifying which of them are true and which fictitious. There are many expeditions enumerated by the biographers which have, in fact, no trustworthy evidence for their support; some are altogether without foundation, and some of them are wrongly termed as expeditions for warring purposes.' The writer in a foot-note adds: 'The biographers have only compiled or arranged the mass of popular romances and favourite tales of campaigns, which had become stereotyped in their time, but were for the most part the inventions of a playful fantasy.' Further, he observes (p. xxii) of Bukhārī's account of Muhammad's wars in the Kitābu-l-Maghāzi: 'Even the latter minimized numbers are not deserving of confidence.'

p. cii. 'It is only the Mohammadan Common Law, with all its traditions or oral sayings of the Prophet—*very few of which are genuine reports*[2]—and the supposed chimerical concurrence of the learned Moslem Doctors, and mostly their analogical reasonings (called *Hadees*, *Ijma*, and *Kias*), passed under the name of *Fiqah* or *Shariat*, that has blended together the spiritual and the secular, and has become a barrier in some respects regarding certain social and political innovations for the higher civilization and progress of the nation.'

[1] Calcutta, 1885, pp. xx ff.

[2] The italics are mine.—A. G.

It is not our purpose to examine how the learned Indian author repudiates traditions and traditionists which do not support his own enlightened views, nor to criticize his attitude towards hadith from the same authorities when they tend to glorify the founder of his religion. But it is interesting to see how the hadith literature, and the vast structure built upon it, are viewed by the modern Muhammadan.[1]

'It is only a theory of our Common Law, in its military and political chapters, which allow[s] waging unprovoked war with non-Moslems, exacting tribute from "the people of the Book", and other idolaters, except those of Arabia, for which the Hanafi Code of the Common Law has nothing short of conversion to Islam or destruction by the sword. As a rule, our canonical legists support their theories by quotations from the Mohammadan Revealed Law, i.e. the Koran, as well as from the Sonnah, or the traditions from the Prophet, however absurd and untenable may be their process of reasoning and argumentative deductions.... The Mohammadan Common Law is by no means divine or superhuman. It mostly consists of uncertain traditions, Arabian usages and customs, some frivolous and fortuitous analogical deductions from the Koran, and a multitudinous array of casuistical sophistry of the canonical legists. It has not been held sacred or unchangeable by enlightened Mohammadans of any Moslem country and in any age since its compilation in the fourth century of the Hejira. All the Mujtahids, 'Ahl Hadis, and other non-Mokallids had had no regard for the four schools of Mohammadan religious jurisprudence, or the Common Law.'

The same writer is even more explicit elsewhere:[2]

[1] *Op. cit.*, pp. 158 ff.

[2] *The proposed political ... reforms in the Ottoman Empire and other Mohammadan States* (Bombay, 1883), pp. xix and 147, quoted by Goldziher, *MS*, p. 132.

'The vast flood of traditions soon formed a chaotic sea. Truth and error, fact and fable mingled together in an undistinguishable confusion. Every religious, social, and political system was defended, when necessary, to please a Khalif or an Ameer to serve his purpose, by an appeal to some oral traditions. The name of Mohammad was abused to support all manner of lies and absurdities, or to satisfy the passion, caprice, or arbitrary will of the despots, leaving out of consideration the creation of any standards of test. . . . I am seldom inclined to quote traditions having little or no belief in their genuineness, as generally they are unauthentic, unsupported, and one-sided.'

It will have become clear how the acute reasoning of this cultured and enlightened Indian gentleman has anticipated many of the conclusions of European Orientalists. His writings are by no means alone in protesting against the authority of tradition. They are symptomatic of a force in liberal Muhammadanism which awaits the opportunity for expression in that Reformation and Renaissance many of the best minds in Islam confidently anticipate.

V

SELECTIONS FROM HADITH

Ethics and morals.—Trade and commercial morality.—Divorce.—Courtesy and kindness.—Slavery.—Treatment of animals.—Retaliation.—Jihād.—Oaths and vows.—Folklore and animism.—Women and marriage.—Manners and customs.

To give an exhaustive account of the whole contents of the hadith literature is as impossible as it is to perform a similar office for the Talmud. The most that can be done in the following pages is to gather under headings some of the salient and some of the more interesting traditions.[1] If the reader finds the constant quotation tedious it must be urged that there are already a large number of books about Islam which give the opinions of their writers; and only by giving the *ipsissima verba* of the traditions can the charge of unfairness and partiality be rebutted.

The moral grandeur and beauty of many of the sayings attributed to Muhammad in the hadith is not the least of the causes of the veneration and affection in which he is held throughout the Muhammadan

[1] I have found the Kanzu-l-'Ummāl impossible to use except as a book of reference. Its vast bulk and peculiar method of arrangement render it unsuitable except as a *corpus traditionum*. Almost all the citations in this chapter are from the *Mishkātu-l-Maṣābīḥ*, Bombay, 1880. The translation of this by Captain A. N. Matthews (Calcutta, 1809), in two volumes, is a remarkable work for its time. A tradition can be readily found by its means, but the work is not complete, or, at any rate, follows a somewhat shorter text, and should be used with caution.

world. And any estimate of his living influence must necessarily be one-sided unless it allows not only for the all-pervading authority and example of the prophet applied as it is to every single detail of human life, but also for the constant expression of a loving and affectionate consideration for mankind. It is this aspect of Islam and of its founder which has not obtained in the West the generous recognition it has earned.

Ethics and Morals. The prophet is said to have declared that 'A Muslim is he from whose tongue and hands Muslims are safe',[1] and that 'it is required of the best of men that they should love God and his apostle above all others and their fellowmen[2] for God's sake'. The prophetic view of honesty as a principle of life is well expressed in the hadith, 'A servant of God shall not acquire property unlawfully and give alms thereof which shall be accepted. Nor shall he spend thereof and be blessed. And he shall not leave it behind him as it will bring him to hell. God does not blot out evil by evil, but God blots out evil by good.'

A chapter bearing the title 'Gentleness in social relations' contains the prayer that God may deal kindly with the man who sells and buys and claims

[1] An interesting play on the word Muslim: *Al muslimu man salima-l-muslimūna* . . .

[2] *'abd.* There is a striking similarity in the phraseology of some of these sayings and the maxims of the great Jewish fathers. The constant enumeration of categories (already found in the book of Proverbs), e.g. Three things are an abomination unto the Lord, is strongly reminiscent of Pirqe Aboth, ed. Taylor, Cambridge, pp. 11–12, &c., as is the use of *'abd* here. Cf. *al tihyu ka-abadim ha-meshammeshim eth ha-Rab*, &c.

his debts in a kindly spirit. 'The place of the faithful merchant who speaks the truth is with the prophets, the veracious, and the martyrs.' The prophet expressly forbade buying from a person in distress; the purchase of any thing to which a risk or hazard attaches;[1] and of fruit before it has ripened. 'He who sells a thing without notifying the buyer of a defect in it will abide in the hate of God, and the angels will curse him unceasingly!' Muhammad is said to have related the following story (which in a shorter and somewhat different form is related of Rabbi Shimʿon in Haggāda): A man of the people who were before you[2] bought a plot of land, and found in it a jar containing gold. Whereupon he said to the seller, 'Take your gold for I only bought your plot.' The latter replied, 'But I sold you the ground and whatever it contained.' So they went to an arbitrator, who instructed them to marry the one's son to the other's daughter and endow them with the proceeds, giving something in alms.

The golden rule is implicitly taught in the following: 'Let no one milk a man's cattle without his permission. Would any one of you like to have his upper chamber broken into, his treasury ransacked, and his food taken away? Now the udders of their cattle are the treasury of their food.' Again: 'There was a man who used to lend money and to say to his servant, "If you come to a man who is unable to pay, pass him over; per-

[1] *baiʿu-l-gharari.* Commentators differ as to the meaning of this phrase.

[2] This reference to the Jews would seem to indicate that the speaker is conscious that he is borrowing from an alien source.

adventure God will pass over our shortcomings." And when he stood before God He did so pass him over.'

This principle is carried even further in the chapter which deals with the laws of retaliation. The higher law of forgiveness is clearly propounded. Abū Dardā says: 'I heard the prophet say, "There is no man who receives a bodily injury and forgives[1] the offender but God will exalt his rank and diminish his sin."'

Trade and Commercial Morality. The following are some of the wholesome restrictions ideally governing the commercial life of the Muhammadan world: Abū Mas'ūd Al Anṣārī said, 'Verily the apostle of God declared unlawful the price of a dog, the wages of immorality, and the fee[2] of a diviner.' Abū Huraira: 'The apostle declared unlawful the price of a dog and the earnings of a singing girl.'

The thoroughness of the prophetic condemnation of usury leaves no room for any part, however indirect, in the transaction. 'The apostle of God cursed the receiver[3] of interest, the payer, the clerk who writes the bond, and the two witnesses thereof, and said, "They are equally culpable."' Another tradition records that Muhammad forbade the barter of a heap of dates of an unknown weight for a specified quantity. Similarly, Muslims are forbidden to sell the fruit upon their trees before it is ripe, even when the two parties are willing to take the risk inseparable from the transaction.[4]

[1] *fataṣaddaqa bihi.* The commentator explains that this means he pardons the offender *ṣabran 'alā qadri-llāh,* leaving requital to Him.

[2] Lit. *douceur.*

[3] Lit. 'eater'. Cf. Hebrew *nāshak,* of biting and of paying interest.

[4] The wisdom of prohibiting speculation in the food supply of a community notorious for its poverty is obvious.

It would seem that the early Muhammadan tradesman was quite modern in his methods. He knew how to 'corner' the food of a town, how to 'doctor' an animal when coping, how to use the arts of misrepresentation in order to squeeze the largest possible sum from his customers. All these immoral methods are sternly condemned in hadith attributed to Muhammad. 'Do not go out to meet the caravans to bargain. . . .[1] Do not buy one against another and outbid one another, and let not the townsman bargain with a Beduin (so as to keep the price up for the consumer). Do not keep back in the teats the milk of a camel or goat.[2] He who buys such a one has the choice, after milking it, of retaining or returning it with a ṣa'a of dates.' 'He who monopolizes a commodity is a sinner.' 'An importer is blessed, but a monopolist is accursed.' 'He who monopolizes food against Muslims may God smite with elephantiasis and grinding poverty.' Another hadith says: 'Though he give the profit in alms it is no atonement.' The charming anthology of prophetic sayings collected by Al Mas'ūdi contains the following, which has as good a claim to be regarded as genuine as those just quoted: 'When he is ruined a merchant speaks the truth!'[3]

Divorce. The Islamic ordinance which makes it impossible for the husband who has divorced his wife by the threefold repetition to remarry her until she has lived with another man is supported by a ruling of the prophet.[4] On the other hand, there are not wanting

[1] I. e. let them come into the markets.

[2] To give the impression that the animal is still yielding milk.

[3] *Op. cit.*, iv, p. 172.

[4] The *Risāla* of Al Kindi, London, 1880, p. 105, contains some

several hadith which make a vigorous protest against such an immoral injunction. Thus, 'Abd Allah b. Mas'ūd reports that the apostle *la'ana-l-muḥallila wa-l-muḥallala lahu* 'cursed the second husband who makes her again lawful for the first and cursed the first husband for whom she was thus made lawful.' Other hadith which remind one of Christ's interpretation of the Mosaic law are: 'Of the things which are lawful the most hateful to God is divorce.' And: 'O Mu'ādh, God has created nothing on the face of the earth dearer to him than the emancipation of slaves, nor anything more hateful to him than divorce.' The following hadith claims to give Muhammad's view on the question of the custody of the child: 'A woman came to the apostle and said, "With my body I carried, nourished, and cradled this son of mine, and now his father has divorced me and wants to snatch him from me." The apostle answered, "You are the most worthy of him so long as you remain unmarried."' On the other hand, two traditions ascribed to Abū Huraira allow the boy to choose which of his parents he will adhere to.[1]

Courtesy and Kindness. The Muslim practice of returning a salutation with an additional compliment or blessing[2] is as old as creation, for at his creation Adam

trenchant observations on this practice from a cultured Christian Arab. The practice was constantly attacked by Christians. Cf. the *Mujādala* of Abū Qurra, MS. Arabe 70, in the Bibliothèque Nationale, fol. 199 b.

[1] For the interpretation of these aqwāl in Muhammadan law see the commentators *in loc.*

[2] For many interesting details see Lane, *Modern Egyptians*, ch. 8. The necessity of replying at length to 'salutations in the market-place' is sometimes objected to by the modern Muslim. An amusing protest

was ordered to go and salute a number of angels and listen to their response, which would be the pattern for posterity. Thereupon he went and said *Al Salām 'alaikum*, and received the response *Al Salām 'alaika wa-raḥmatu-llāhi*.

A long section of the hadith literature is full of sayings inculcating the necessity of kindliness and love, of which the following may serve as examples: 'God will not have compassion on him who hath not compassion on mankind.' 'The Compassionate has compassion on those who show compassion. Show compassion to those on earth, and He who is in Heaven will have compassion on you.' 'For every young man who honours an old man on account of his age will God ordain one who will honour him in his old age.' 'The best house amid the Muslim community is that which contains an orphan who is well treated; and the worst is that wherein an orphan is wronged.' 'He who is destitute of gentleness is destitute of goodness.'

Hospitality, for which the Arabs have ever been justly praised, is in hadith a mark of the true believer. Thus, Abū Huraira tells us that the prophet said: 'Whoever believes in God and the last day, let him honour his guest, let him not injure his neighbour, and if he has nothing good to say let him remain silent.' A more precise definition of the hospitality incumbent on a Muslim: 'Whosoever believes in God and the last day let him entertain his guest bountifully for a day and a night. Hospitality (should be given) for three

against this genial practice appeared in one of the Cairene newspapers in 1918 under the heading of 'Izzē ek'.

days. What is done over and above that is in the nature of almsgiving. It is not right for a guest to stay in a man's house so long as to embarrass him.'

Again, Abu-l-Ahwas asks the prophet whether he is to entertain a man who in the past had refused him hospitality. Muhammad replies, 'Certainly, entertain him.'

Slavery. The status of the slave in the Muhammadan world does not differ materially from that described in the New Testament. As a co-religionist of his master he is a member of the household, and shares in the fortune good or bad of his owner.[1] The following sayings will illustrate the traditional policy and attitude of Muslims towards their slaves: 'The slave must be given food and clothing. He must not be given a task which he is unable to perform.' 'It is your brethren that God has put beneath your hands. He who has one thus subjected to him by God must feed him from what he eats himself, and clothe him in

[1] A good deal of misapprehension still exists in this country as to the lot of slaves in Islam. It may be doubted whether it is so unenviable as that of many people in our great cities. Cf. Burton, *Pilgrimage*, i, London, 1915, p. 61, and Doughty, *Arabia Deserta*, i, pp. 554–5. 'In those Africans there is no resentment that they have been made slaves . . . even though cruel men-stealers rent them from their parentage. The patrons who paid their price have adopted them into their households, the males are circumcised, and—that which enfranchises their souls, even in the long passion of home-sickness—God has visited them in their mishap; they can say, 'It was his grace', since they be thereby entered into the saving religion. This, therefore, they think is the better country, where they are the Lord's free men, a land of more civil life, the soil of the two Sanctuaries, the land of Muhammad: for such they do give God thanks that their bodies were sometime sold into slavery!'

his own clothes. He must not give him a task beyond his strength. If he does, then he must help him himself.' Again, 'He who beats a slave for a fault he has not committed or slaps his face must make atonement by setting him free.' 'Whoso separates a woman from her child (the commentator explains, by selling, giving, &c.) God will separate him from his loved ones on the resurrection day.' It is related that the apostle of God gave Ali a slave, saying: 'Do not beat him, for I have ordered that those who pray shall not be beaten, and I have seen this slave at prayer.' The chapter on Qiṣāṣ contains the words of the prophet, 'We will slay him who slays his slave, and we will maim him who maims him.' (Another version reads: 'We will castrate him who castrates his slave.' [1])

Treatment of Animals. The claims of the brute creation on the compassion of good Muslims is clearly set forth. The prophet once passed by a camel whose belly clave to its back. 'Fear God', said he, 'in these dumb animals, and ride them when they are fit to be ridden, and let them go free when it is meet they should rest.' The following of kindness to birds: We were on a journey with the apostle of God, who left us for a short space. We saw a ḥummara with its two young, and took the young birds. The ḥummara hovered with fluttering wings, and the prophet returned,

[1] The hatred of the right-minded Muslim for the practice of making eunuchs is expressed by Al Jāḥiẓ, who, while unfairly blaming Christians for originating this horrible custom, rightly asks how they dare claim a monopoly of kindness and tenderness and yet habitually commit this crime. Muslim historians often note with disapproval that the Umayyads were the first to introduce this barbarity into Islam.

saying, 'Who has injured this bird by taking its young? Return them to her.' Again: Do not clip the fore-locks of your horses, nor their manes, nor their tails; for the tail is their fly-whisk; the mane is their covering; and the forelock has good fortune bound within it.[1]

Animals are not to be ridden unnecessarily. By precept and example the prophet showed consideration for beasts of burden. Thus Abū Huraira reports that he said: 'Do not use the backs of your beasts as pulpits, for God has only made them subject to you in order that they may bring you to a town you could only otherwise reach by fatigue of body.'[2] . . . While Anas writing of his custom says: 'When we stopped at a halt we did not say our prayers until we had unburdened the camels.' Nevertheless a donkey may be made to carry two men, for we read that Buraida said: 'While the apostle of God was walking a man with a donkey came up, and said as he moved back on the donkey's rump: "Ride, O apostle of God." He replied: "No, for you are more worthy of riding in front on your own beast, unless you give me the place." He said: "I do give you the place;" so he rode in front.'

The Law of Retaliation. The Quran has established

[1] This is one of the sayings of the heathen Arabs which was incorporated in the hadith literature. Cf. *Imru-l-Qais*, 8, 1. Muhammad himself did not scruple to incorporate sayings and proverbs of the *Jāhiliyya* in the Quran, so that his followers had a precedent for drawing on this source.

[2] The commentator says, 'The meaning is: Do not sit on their backs, and make them stand while you transact your business; but dismount, accomplish your object, and then ride them again.'

in the Islamic community the principle of 'an eye for an eye and a tooth for a tooth', and, like its predecessor in this legislation, the Torah of Moses, it claims divine authority for its law. Nevertheless, the Muslim, like the Jew, knows how to interpret this law with justice and some degree of mildness. The hadith illustrate the application of the principle, and an attempt to carry it through in opposition to the deeply-rooted custom of paying and receiving pecuniary compensation for bodily injuries. Thus Anas: A Jew broke the head of a slave girl between two stones. She was asked the name of the culprit, and when the Jew's name was mentioned she made a sign with the head in assent. So the Jew was brought, and acknowledged the act; whereupon the apostle ordered that his head should be broken with a stone.

The same authority reports that Rubaiʿ, the aunt of Anas b. Mālik, broke the teeth of a slave girl of the Anṣār. They came to the prophet, and he ordered the law of qiṣāṣ to be applied to her. Anas b. Al Naḍr said, 'No, by God, her teeth shall not be broken, O apostle of God.' He said, 'But, Anas, retaliation is in the Book of God!' Then the people agreed to accept the price of an injury, and the prophet said: 'There are some servants of God who, if they take an oath by God, God holds them free from guilt.'[1]

Again: He who kills a man intentionally must be given up to the relatives of the slain: if they wish they can kill him, and if they will they can accept blood-money. There are only three crimes for which a man

[1] The commentator writes, The meaning is: 'God makes him truthful in his oath, not a perjurer', i. e. God performs, or allows him to perform, his oath.

can be condemned to death according to the hadith, namely, wilful murder, adultery, and apostasy from Islam. The murder of Muslims is, of course, in question, as the chapter on Jihād clearly shows, though harsh treatment of adherents of other faiths is deprecated. The interesting point is raised: At what point can a man rightly be regarded as a Muslim? The prophet was asked: 'If I meet an unbeliever and we fight, and he smites off my hand with his sword, and then takes refuge behind a tree, and says, "I am a Muslim to God" (another version is: And when I am about to kill him he says, "There is no God but the God"), am I to kill him after that?' He replied, 'Do not kill him.' 'But, O prophet of God,' said the man, 'he has cut off one of my hands.' The apostle answered: 'Do not kill him, for if you kill him, before you can kill him he is in your state, and you are in the state[1] he was before he made his utterance.'

It will be obvious that the example given is one evolved from the inventive minds of the Muhammadan legists. It is closely akin to the discussions of the Jewish halāka, and owes it origin to the desire to frame traditions which will give the weight of sacred authority to every possible contingency of life.[2] As though it were realized that it would be neither safe nor practicable to allow an enemy to escape death in action by the mere repetition of the formula *la ilāha illa-llāh*, the foregoing tradition is weakened somewhat in its effect by the tradition attributed to Usāma b. Zaid.

[1] You cannot kill him because he has become a Muslim, and to kill a Muslim is to commit murder and forfeit your own life. If you do kill, you have come under God's wrath like an infidel.

[2] Cf. Margoliouth, *Early Development*, p. 96.

'The apostle of God sent us against some of the Juhaina, and I was about to spear one of them when he cried, "There is no God but the God." I transfixed and slew him, and when I came to the prophet and told him what I had done he said: "Did you kill him when he had borne witness in these words?" I replied, "But, apostle of God, he only did that to save himself from death!" Muhammad said: "Can it be that you did not test his sincerity?"' (Another version is: 'What will you do with those words: "There is no God but the God" at the day of judgement?' The prophet repeated these words several times.)

The following hadith expresses the opinion of the religious on the murder of an unoffending non-Muslim. 'Whoso slays a *Mu'āhid* shall not smell the scent of Paradise; and verily its perfume is perceptible a forty years' journey distant.' Abū Dardā expresses the higher truth when he says: 'There is no man who receives a bodily injury and forgives the offender, but God will exalt his rank and lessen his sin.'

Theft. Theft, according to ancient tradition, is to be punished by the amputation of the hand. According to 'Āisha the prophet said that this punishment was not to be inflicted unless the theft amounted to the fourth of a dinar. Abū Huraira, however, says: 'God curses a thief who steals an egg or a rope, and his hand must be cut off.'[1]

Jihād. So many Christian writers have discussed

[1] Various attempts have been made by the commentators to mitigate the harshness of this doctrine. Thus, it is said, *baiḍa* means an iron helmet, and *ḥabl* a ship's cable! Others think it refers to primitive practice. The *Qibla*, the organ of the Sharīf of Mecca, August, 1918, contains an account of the application of the Sharia' to a local thief.

at length the prominence assigned to Jihād, the holy war against infidels incumbent upon all Muslims, that it does not seem necessary to quote here more than a few of the exceedingly large number of traditions on this subject. From these it will be seen that fighting in the way of God (*fī sabīli-'llāh*) is a religious exercise of supreme merit, dearer in the sight of God than any other form of piety: the meanest participator—the non-combatant—who loses his life or substance in the holy war is thereby assured of eternal life.

The most extravagant praise of *Jihād* is the saying vouched by Sahal b. Sa'd, and recorded by Bukhārī: 'Frontier duty for one day in the way of God is better than the world and all that therein is.' This tradition in almost the same words is independently ascribed to Anas. A man asked if his sins would be forgiven if he fell fighting in the way of God. Muhammad answered, 'Yes, if you display enduring patience, faith in a future reward, ever advance and never retreat. This does not apply to the sin of debt. Gabriel informed me of this.' 'One of the Companions travelled by a mountain path in which was a pool of sweet water; and liking it exceedingly he exclaimed, "Would that I might withdraw from men and dwell in this spot!" The apostle of God was told of this, and said: "Do not so, for to remain in the way of God is better than praying in one's house for seventy years. Do you not desire that God should pardon you and bring you into Paradise? Make raids in the way of God! He that contends in the way of God but the time between two milkings of a camel, paradise is his due."'

Al Tirmidhī and Ibn Māja report the following:

the martyr has six privileges with God: his sins are pardoned when the first drop of blood falls; he is shown his seat in paradise; he is safe from the punishment of the grave and secure from the great terror (i.e. hell); a crown of dignity is placed on his head one jewel of which is worth more than the world and all that is therein; and he is married to seventy dark-eyed virgins; and he makes successful intercession for seventy of his relatives. 'He who equips a warrior in the way of God has fought himself; and he who is left behind to take care of a warrior's family has fought himself.'

The last quoted hadith probably marks an early stage in the reaction against the extravagant claims of martyrs on the admiration of men and the notice of God. Taken by themselves the hadith we have selected clearly imply that the martyr's merit exceeds that of all others. But inasmuch as all men could not be combatants, even in the early days of the Arabian Caliphate, rival traditions soon began to circulate, asserting that the warrior had no better chance of eternal life than the pious non-combatant. Of these perhaps the most significant is fathered on the long-suffering Abū Huraira: 'He who believes in God and his apostle and performs prayer and keeps the fast of Ramaḍan has a claim on God to be brought into Paradise, whether he fights in the way of God or sits in his plot on which he was born.' They said: 'Then are we to tell men of this?' Muhammad answered: 'There are in paradise a hundred steps which God has prepared for his warriors: the space between two steps is as the space between heaven and earth. When you pray ask for *Firdaus*, for that is in the middle of paradise (*Al Janna*) and its highest point: above it is the throne of the Merciful. From it gush forth the rivers of paradise.' This tradition would seem to recognize a protest registered against the prevailing exaltation of martyrdom, and at the same time reinforces the claim of the warrior by giving him a position in paradise above that of the faithful. There is a sturdy independence about the first half of the tradition which creates a strong suspicion that the second half has been added by those who feared the logical application of its teaching. The next stage is clear. It is asserted that he who asks God with all sincerity to grant him martyrdom will have the reward of the martyr though he die upon his bed. The object of this hadith is apparently to safeguard, as it were, the interests of the man who has fought in the *Jihād* unscathed, or has been prevented by some unavoidable circumstance from taking any part in it. Abū Huraira is the spokesman in the last stage of the controversy between the soldier and the civilian for priority in paradise: were it not for the terrible seriousness of the *Jihād* itself the conclusion would be laughable. 'The apostle of God said: "Whom do you regard as a martyr?" The companions replied: "He who is killed in the way of God." He replied: "Of a truth in that case the martyrs of my people would be few. . . . He who dies in the way of God (without being slain) is a martyr, as also he who dies of the plague and of a disease of the belly."'

Oaths and vows. It can hardly be said that an oath or a vow among Muslims has the binding force even on the pious that it assumes in the West. The hadith, as will appear from the few extracts given below, practically make the performance of a vow dependent on the convenience of the speaker. This does not mean that a vow has no power to bind; but rather that there is an instinctive dislike to a vow of any kind. When made it need not be regarded as irrevocable.[1] Vow not at all is the sum of the traditions recorded in the *Bābu-l-Nudhūr* of the *Mishkātu-l-Maṣābīḥ*; and the chapter heading in the *Sunan* of Ibn Māja *Al Nahyu 'ani-l-nadhr*[2] speaks for itself. It is related that during the *Khuṭba* the prophet saw a man standing, and asked the reason. He was told that the man had vowed never to sit, nor seek shade, nor speak, and to fast. Thereupon the prophet gave orders that he was to abandon his intention. A similar incident is narrated of an old man whom Muhammad saw tottering along between his two sons, and was told that he had vowed a vow to walk to the Ka'ba. Said he: 'Verily God the exalted does not need that this man should punish himself!' and he ordered him to ride. Ka'b said to the apostle, 'It is a part of my penitence that I should strip myself of my wealth in alms to God and his apostle.' The apostle answered, 'Keep back some of your money, for it will be better for you.' I said, 'I will retain my lot in the ground in Khaibar.' Again: 'When you take an oath to do a thing, and you see a better alternative, then do what is best and make atonement for your oath.' 'Āisha said: This verse was revealed: 'God will not punish you for rashness in your oaths,[3] as for example when a man says, "No, by God!" and "Yea, by God!"'

[1] Al Fakhrī (ed. Derenbourg, pp. 267 f.) will illustrate the care that is necessary to devise an oath that will bind a Muslim when anything of great importance is at stake.

[2] Prohibition of Vows.

[3] Sur. ii. 226.

The *Bābu-l-Amān* of the *Mishkāt* contains some interesting hadith on the subject of fidelity to private and national agreements made between belligerents; they display a high standard of honour. 'An agreement lay between Mu'āwiya and Rūm, and he used to march to the frontier so that, when the agreement expired, he might raid them. There came a man on horseback, crying, Allāhu Akbar! Allāhu Akbar! Fidelity, not Treachery! When they looked they saw it was 'Amr b. 'Abasata. On being asked what he meant, he said: "I heard the apostle of God say: 'Whoso has an agreement with people must not break it until the allotted time has passed or give notice dissolving the agreement on equal terms.' So Mu'āwiya withdrew with his men."' This tradition, as the mention of Mu'āwiya's pious obedience would suggest, is not to be found in the Ṣaḥīḥān, though both Tirmidhī and Abū Dāūd report it. Again, 'The apostle said to two men who came to him from Musailama,[1] "By God, were it not that messengers (i.e. heralds) must not be killed I would behead you."'

Folk-lore and Animism. The hadith literature contains a very large number of allusions to pre-Islamic practices. Besides the well-known heathen rites of the pilgrimage to the holy places,[2] we find the beliefs of the pagan predecessors of Muhammad often confirmed by him, and their customs and prejudices repeated.[3] Along with these primitive folk-

[1] The false prophet. Muir, *Life of Muhammad*, p. 478.

[2] Burton, *Pilgrimage*, pp. 279–93.

[3] A most interesting account of the extent of animistic beliefs and customs in Islam to-day will be found in Zwemer's *The Influence of Animism on Islam*, London, 1920.

lore is perpetuated. Examples are: 'The cry of a child at birth is caused by the evil touch of Satan.'[1] 'The apostle said to his Companions, "When your brethren were slain in the day of Uḥud God put their spirits into the crops of green birds which come down to the rivers of paradise and eat of its fruit and shelter in golden chandeliers suspended in the shadow of God's throne. And when they perceive the excellence of their food, their drink, and their resting-place they exclaim: 'Who will inform our brethren of our state in paradise, so that they may not despise it and refrain from war?' God said, 'I will inform them of you,' and He revealed: 'Reckon not those slain in the way of God as dead. Verily they live', &c."' (Sur. iii. 170).[2]

Snakes. 'Kill snakes; kill the one with two black lines on its back and the *abtar*,[3] for these two blind the sight and cause miscarriage.' 'Abd Allah said: 'While I was driving out a snake to kill it Abū Labāba called out to me, "Do not kill it." I said, "But the apostle ordered snakes to be killed." He replied, "Yes, but afterwards he forbade the killing of those who live in houses, seeing they are inhabitants."' The commentator here explains that the passage means that the snakes are jinn. Zwemer remarks,[4] 'The superstitious idea that every house has a serpent guardian is pretty general throughout the country [Egypt], and many families still provide a bowl of milk for their serpent

[1] This superstition is nearly as old as man.

[2] The student will find a somewhat similar belief, cited as a belief of the heathen Arabs, in Shahrastānī, *Kitabu-l-Milal wa-l-Niḥal*, ed. Cureton, p. 433.

[3] i.e. short-tailed.

[4] *Op. cit.*, p. 224.

protector, believing that calamity would come upon them if the serpent were neglected. This is undoubtedly a survival of the ancient belief that the serpent was the child of the earth—the oldest inhabitant of the land and guardian of the ground.'

Perhaps a clearer example of the power ascribed to the snake is: 'These houses have domestic snakes; if you see one of them urge it to go three times. If it goes, well; if not, then kill it, for it is an infidel.' Again: 'If a serpent appears in a dwelling say to it: "We ask you by the agreement with Noah[1] and Solomon b. David not to stay and annoy us." If it returns then kill it.' It is not surprising that those who did not share the animistic beliefs of the composers of the hadith just quoted display no tenderness towards the snake in traditions coined to express a more enlightened view. Ibn 'Abbās says: 'The prophet ordered snakes to be killed, and said, Whoso lets one alone fearing the vengeance of his mate is not of us.' Similarly, Abū Huraira is made to voice the common sense view: 'Never have we made peace with them since war between man and snake began, and whoso lets one of them alone out of fear is not of us.'

Jinn and Devils. 'Verily Satan is present in all the activities of life, even at meals, so when one of you drops a mouthful he must remove any dirt from it, and then eat it, not leaving it to Satan. And when he has finished, he must lick his fingers, for he does not know in what part of his food blessing resides.'

[1] The naïve suggestion of the commentator as to the date of this agreement is that perhaps it was made when Noah took the snakes into the ark!

The *jinn* are of three kinds: one has wings and flies, serpents and dogs are another, and the third stops at a place and travels about.[1] 'At the beginning of nightfall keep your little ones in, for Satan (commentator, i.e. the *jinn*) roams abroad at that time. When an hour of the night has passed let them free. And bolt your doors and make mention of the name of God. Satan cannot open a door which has been bolted. Tie the necks of your water skins, and mention the name of God, and put a veil over your waterpots, mentioning His name (though you but lay something across them), and extinguish your lamps.'

'When you hear the barking of dogs or the braying of asses at night then seek refuge in God from Satan the stoned, for animals see what is invisible to you, and forbear to go out often when the feet are at rest (i.e. at night). For God in the night spreads abroad whom he will of his creatures.' (The conclusion of this hadith follows fairly closely the text of the preceding.) Again, of the noise of bells we read: 'A slave girl took Ibn Zubair's daughter to 'Umar. She had little bells on her leg, and 'Umar cut them off, with the words: "I heard the apostle of God say there is a devil with every bell."' When any one sees a vision (or dreams a dream) which he dislikes let him

[1] The same extreme vagueness about the *jinn* in the mind of the modern Beduin is noticed by Doughty, *Arabia Deserta*. I have no doubt that the Jewish view of *Shēdim* has influenced the Arab writer (unless we seek a common origin in Persia). *Talm. Chagīga*, 16 a: 'Six things are said of the demons: in three they resemble the ministering angels, and in three they resemble the sons of men. As angels they have wings, and fly from one end of the world to the other, and they know what the future holds in store. . . . As men, they eat and drink, they reproduce their species, and they die.'

spit to the left three times, and take refuge with God from Satan three times, and let him turn from the side on which he lay when he dreamed.

Spells and the evil eye. There is no attempt in the hadith to disguise the source of popular beliefs which are still held by the ignorant and superstitious to-day. Thus 'Auf b. Mālik Al Ashjā'ī says: 'We were in the habit of using spells in the time of ignorance, and we said: "O apostle of God what is your opinion of them?" He replied: "Show me your spells. There is no harm in a spell in which there is no taint of polytheism (*shirk*)."'

Anas reports that the prophet permitted the use of spells against the evil eye, snake-bite, and pustules. On one occasion he saw a slave-girl suffering from a stroke of Satan (i.e. jaundice), and said: 'Use spells for her, for the evil eye has looked upon her.'[1] Jābir relates that Muhammad had forbidden spells, and the family of 'Amr b. Ḥazm came and said: 'We have a spell for use on those bitten by scorpions, and you have forbidden spells'; and they showed him it. He answered: 'I see no harm in it. If any of you can help his brother by it, let him.' The theistic view of such charms is expressed in hadith, of which these must serve as examples: Īsa b. Ḥamza said: 'I went to visit 'Abd Allah b. 'Ukaim, who suffered from a rash, and said: "Why do you not tie on a charm?" "God forbid," said he, "for the prophet of God said, 'He who depends on a thing will be left trusting to it.'" "It will suffice you to say what the apostle of God used to say: 'Take away misfortune,

[1] The Nihāya explains the words *bihā naẓratun* thus: bihā 'ainun aṣabathā min naẓari-l-jinni.

O Lord of men, and heal. Thou art the Healer: there is no healing but Thy healing.'"'

Omens. 'The prophet used to take good omens, not bad ones, and he was fond of a happy name.' 'Taking a bad omen is polytheism. These words Muhammad said thrice. There is not one of us but will have evil presentiments removed by God if he trust in Him.'

Divination. The following hadith make it evident that traditionists have no doubt that sorcerers and diviners are able to foretell the future.[1] The general conclusion is that they obtain their information from the evil one and his messengers. The first of those quoted is interesting, as the somewhat cryptic reference to the prophet who used to write suggests a reference to John viii. 6.[2]

Mu'āwīya b. Al Ḥakam said: 'I said to the apostle of God, "In the time of ignorance we used to resort to diviners." He said: "Do not consult them." "Also we drew bad omens." He replied: "If you are troubled in your mind because of it do not let it deter you from your purpose." "We used to draw lines."[3] He said: "One of the prophets used to draw lines. And he whose writing agrees with his is good."'

From 'Āisha. When the prophet was asked about diviners, he said, 'They are nothing.' 'But', they objected, 'it sometimes happens that they relate what

[1] *v. s.*

[2] For a description of the writing of incantations, &c., see Lane, *op. cit.*, pp. 274 ff.

[3] Probably on the ground (though the word used is khaṭṭ, not nakata).

is true.' He said: 'That word of truth the jinn seizes and repeats in the ear of his devotee[1] . . . and they mix more than a hundred lies with it.' Again: 'The angels descend in rainclouds and mention what has been decreed in heaven. Then the devils listen stealthily and reveal what has been said to diviners, and they add a hundred lies to it out of their own minds.' Ḥafṣa reports that Muhammad said: 'He who goes to a sorcerer ('arrāf) to ask about a matter, his prayer will not be accepted for forty days.' 'He who learns knowledge from the stars learns a branch of sorcery (*siḥr*) the more of one the more of the other.'

The following is the explanation of the shooting stars. 'While some of the Companions were sitting with the prophet one night a star shot and gleamed bright. "What used you to say in the time of ignorance," said he, "when a star shot like that?" They replied: "God and his apostle know best. We used to say: 'A great man is born to-night and a great man has died.'" He said: "It did not shoot for the death or the birth of any one, but when your Lord decrees a thing the bearers of the Throne praise God; then the inhabitants of heaven near thereto, until the

[1] The reading and meaning of the two words omitted are doubtful—qarra-l-dajājati—qarra, according to the *Nihāya*, means to repeat or pour words into a person's ear until he understands them. The commentator mentions that qarra is the verb used when a hen brings her cackling to an end. He records a variant zujāja, and infers 'the jinn pours it into his ear as one pours liquid into a glass bottle!' Ibn Al Ṣalāḥ says the former reading is correct, and the latter corrupt. I suspect an ancient corruption. 'As a hen repeats' is hardly a satisfactory sense. Houdas, *op. cit.*, iv, p. 84, completely ignores the words in text and notes.

Tasbīḥ reaches the inhabitants of this lowest heaven. Those near ask the bearers of the throne what their Lord has said. They are informed, and the inhabitants of heaven inquire one of another until the information reaches this lowest heaven, and the *jinn* steal the tidings and carry (throw) it to their devotees and (the stars) are thrown at them."'[1]

Again: 'God created these stars for three reasons: to be an ornament of the sky, to be used as stones against the devils, and as signs to guide people. Whoso interprets them otherwise is in error, loses his good fortune, and pretends to know what he is ignorant of.'

'There is no contagious disease, nor ornithomancy, nor *hāma*, nor significance in the serpent Ṣafar.[2] Nevertheless, flee from one with elephantiasis as you would from a lion.' An Arab of the desert said: 'O Apostle of God, what of the camels in the desert? they are as it were gazelles in condition,

[1] Cf. Suras, 15. 17; 18. 48; 37. 7; and 26. 212. This explanation of the phenomenon caused considerable embarrassment when Greek astronomy and philosophy gained a strong position among Arabian savants. Cf. Al Jāḥiẓ, *in loc.*, and Margoliouth, *Early Development*, pp. 226 ff.

[2] Text: *lā ʿadwā walā ṭīrata wa lā hāmata wa lā ṣafara.* This hadith is cited by the author of the *Mustatraf* and by Shahrastānī, *op. cit.*, p. 433. In the latter quotation the author might possibly have taken ʿadwā to refer to metempsychosis. The passages quoted will explain the *hāma* or bird which issued from a dead man's skull. Ṣafar means either the month of that name, or a kind of serpent. The commentator of the *Mishkāt* (p. 383) says: *kānū yatashā 'amūna bi-dukhūli Ṣafar.* They used to regard the entry of a Ṣafar as an evil omen. Houdas, *op. cit.*, iv, p. 83, writes: 'Suivant les uns, il s'agirait d'un animal, sorte de serpent ou de ver, logé dans le corps de l'homme; il mordrait les entrailles de l'homme chaque fois que celles-ci seraient vides et qu'il aurait faim.' See *Mishkāt*, margin.

yet mix them with mangy camels, and they become mangy too.' The apostle answered: 'But who infected the first with a contagious disease?' The shrewd criticism levelled at this doctrine by the Beduin is met by a reply which evades the point either by referring the disaster to an act of God decreed and unavoidable, or by attributing the disease to the cause responsible for the first outbreak, and therefore not dependent on the infected camels. In either case this is yet another example of the inability of the Oriental to distinguish between a primary and a secondary cause.[1]

The comparative paucity of personal names in Muhammadan countries is due to the influence of traditions which express God's approval of certain names, or the prophet's taste in such matters. Thus Anas tells us that when Muhammad was in the market a man called out, 'Ho Abu-l-Qāṣim!' and the prophet turned towards him. 'I merely called this fellow,' said the man, whereupon the prophet said: 'Call your children by my name, but do not use my *kunya*.' 'God likes best the names 'Abd Allah and 'Abdu-l-Raḥmān.' 'The vilest of names before God at the day of resurrection will be maliku-l-amlāk (king of kings).'

[1] On this Al Suyūṭī, quoted by Lane, *Arabian Society*, says: 'A Halīmī says, "Communicable or contagious diseases are six: small-pox, measles, itch or scab, foul breath or putridity, melancholy(!) and pestilential maladies; and diseases engendered are also six: leprosy, hectic, epilepsy, gout, elephantiasis, and phthisis." But this does not contradict the saying of the prophet, "There is no transition of diseases by contagion or infection . . .", for the transition here meant is one occasioned by the disease itself; whereas the effect is of God, who causes pestilence to spread when there is intercourse with the diseased.' Thus is responsibility moved to the predestination of God.

An unsuccessful attempt on the part of Muhammad to change a name he did not like is recorded by Bukhārī. Saʿīd b. Al Musayyib related that his grandfather Ḥazn went to the prophet, who asked his name. 'Ḥazn,' he was told. 'No, you are Sahl,' said he. My grandfather said: 'I am not going to change a name my father gave me.' Saʿīd added: 'From that time hardness in temperament has continued in my family.'

Women and Marriage. Much has been written on the status of women in Islam, and the theologian must decide how far responsibility for the present state of affairs rests, on the one hand, with Islam as a system, and with sinful human nature on the other. The hadith in this, as in so many other matters, reflect the thoughts of the best and the worst minds. For instance, Muhammad, as reported by ʿAbd Allah b. ʿUmar, tells us: 'The world, all of it is property,[1] and the best property in the world is a virtuous woman.' And again, as reported by Abū Huraira: 'A woman may be married for four things: her money, her birth, her beauty, and her religion. Get thou a religious woman (otherwise) may thy hands be rubbed in dirt!'

On the other hand, Usāma b. Zaid would have us know that the apostle said: 'I have not left behind me a source of discord[2] more injurious to men than women.' And Ibn ʿUmar: 'A woman, a house, and a horse are bad omens.'

[1] The meaning of this word *matāʿ* is a little doubtful. It might mean 'enjoyable' or 'valuable'. Professor Margoliouth, who reminds me of the reference to Sur. iii. 12, inclines to agree with my rendering above.

[2] *fitna.* The *Nihāya* explains *fattān: muḍillu-l-nāsa ʿan il-haqq,* 'a fattān is one who causes men to err from the truth'.

As to the subordination of the wife to the husband: 'A Muslim must not hate his wife. If he dislikes her for one trait let him find pleasure in another.' 'If a man summon his wife to his bed and she refuse to come, so that he spends the night in anger, the angels curse her till morning.' (Another version of this says: 'He who is in heaven is enraged against her till her husband is pleased with her.')

Lastly, a tradition—which must either be officially repudiated or for ever condemn the system which enshrines it—resting on the authority of Mu'ādh: 'Whenever a woman vexes her husband in this world, his wife among the *ḥuris* of Paradise says: "Do not vex him (May God slay thee!) for he is only a guest with thee. He will soon leave thee and come to us."'[1]

Political power may sometimes be held by women, but the prophetic verdict on women in high places is recorded by Bukhārī thus: 'When the apostle of God was informed that the Persians had made Kisra's daughter their sovereign, he exclaimed: "A people that entrusts its affairs to a woman will never prosper."'

The subordinate position of women in the religious life is likewise fixed by the Prophet's utterance. 'He went out on the day of the victims and Bairam to the place of prayer, and passing some women he said: "O company of women give alms, for I have seen that

[1] It is only fair to say that this tradition, which is recorded by Ibn Māja and Al Tirmidhī, is marked *gharīb* by the latter. At the same time, it is a logical inference from the Quran itself that if Muslims in paradise are to be gratified by the possession of *huris* there will be no place for their wives of this world. A great point is made of this by the Christian disputant at the court of Mā'mūn, see Paris MS. Arabe, no. 70, fol. 7.

many of you will be inhabitants of hell." "Why?" said they. Replied he: "Because you curse much and deny the kindness of husbands. I have not seen—despite your deficiency in intelligence and religion—any sharper than you in captivating the mind of the resolute." They said: "What is the defect in our religion and intelligence?" He answered: "Is not the witness of a woman equal to half the witness of a man? This is the defect in her intelligence. And when she is ceremonially impure she neither prays nor fasts. This is the defect in her religion."'[1]

Manners and Customs. No more than a mere selection of the vast number of traditions enshrining the customs of the Arabs in the time of Muhammad and some of those which have grown up in the Muhammadan world in the centuries following the prophet's death can be given here. Some of those selected will serve to show what a tremendous conservative force hadith has been through the centuries, preserving among the various nations of Islam the habits of primitive Muslims. It will be seen that the action of the modern Muhammadan in adopting European dress marks not a mere change from an Oriental to an Occidental tailor, but a break with an apostolic past, similar in gravity to that made by Hellenistic Jews in the Seleucid era, and often entailing similar consequences.[2] Others will show how customs unknown to early Muhammadans were borrowed from the superior culture of the Greeks and Persians, the memory of the old conservative Arab recording their

[1] Cf. *Talmud*, sub *Niddah*.

[2] E. Bevan, *Jerusalem under the High Priests*, pp. 35 ft.

alien origin. The inclusion of a few here can only be justified by their strangeness, curious character, or dogmatic foundation.

Muslims are enjoined to eat without a knife, following the example of their prophet. 'Meat was brought to the apostle of God and the shoulder was put before him, he being fond of the shoulder, and he ate of it with his teeth.' More explicitly as a command from him: 'Do not cut meat with a knife as foreigners do, but bite it with the teeth. It tastes better, and is more wholesome thus.'

The habit of drinking water while standing is evidently disliked and to be avoided,[1] though the hadith do not speak with one voice: thus Anas says, 'The apostle forbade a man to drink while standing'; and Abū Huraira underlines the prohibition, 'Let none of you drink water while standing, and if any one forgets, he must vomit it forth.' On the contrary, Ibn 'Abbās says: 'I brought to the prophet a bucket of zamzam water, and he drank of it while standing'; and Ibn 'Umar: 'In the time of the apostle of God we used to eat while walking and drink while standing.'[2] And yet another tradition relates that the prophet was seen to drink standing and sitting.

A good example of the way in which custom was perpetuated is to be found in the following narrative: 'Ibn 'Umar passed by the apostle of God, and his drawers were slack. The latter said, "Raise them," and again, "Further." "Afterwards," said Ibn 'Umar, "I strove to keep them thus." Some people asked, "How far up?" He said, "To the middle of my

[1] Burton, *Pilgrimage*, p. 6, and *v. s.*

[2] Tirmidhī marks this hadith as *ḥasan, ṣaḥīḥ, gharīb.*

shanks."' More extravagantly Abū Huraira: 'The portion of the drawers below the ankles is hell fire!'[1]

False hair is not to be worn, for Muhammad said: 'God curse the woman who wears false hair and the woman who ties it on.' Gold rings are not to be worn, though silver ones are permissible. They should be carried on the little finger according to some authorities. The following two hadith are of interest, in that popular custom proved too strong for them, and they are therefore abrogated (*mansūkh*). Asma bint Yazīd: 'The woman who wears a golden necklace will have one of hell fire fastened to her neck on the day of resurrection.' A similar threat is directed against gold ear-rings. Ḥudhaifa's sister: 'O women, can you not be adorned with silver? Every one of you that is bedecked with gold and shows it shall be punished.'

The march of civilization bringing customs unknown in the simplicity of patriarchal Arabian society is admitted and accepted in the following: Anas said, 'I do not know that the prophet ever saw fine bread to the day of his death; nor did he see a goat baked (in its skin, adds the commentator).' Sahal b. Sa'd said: 'The apostle of God never saw sifted flour from the time God sent him forth on his mission until He took him to Himself; nor did he ever see a sieve.'

One of the edicts of the prophets which has had an incalculable effect on the culture, art, and architecture of the Muhammadan East is his ban on pictures. 'Angels will not enter a house containing a dog or pictures.' 'Āisha relates that she bought a cushion on which were pictures, and when the apostle of God

[1] According to the commentator it means the wearer will go to hell. See Lane, *ME*, p. 30.

saw them he stood at the door and would not enter. Seeing signs of displeasure in his face she said: 'O apostle of God, I repent unto God and his apostle. What have I done amiss?' He asked, 'What is the meaning of this cushion?' 'I bought it for you to sit and recline on,' said she. 'Verily,' he answered, 'the makers of these pictures will be severely punished on the day of resurrection, and it will be said to them, "Bring to life the pictures you have made."'[1] Again, 'Every painter will be in hell.'

It is said that a man came to Ibn 'Abbās and lamented that he had lost his livelihood, for he lived by his painting. What was he to do? 'Woe to you,' says he, 'if you must needs paint, then paint trees and objects that have not a spirit in them.'

There is little reason to doubt that this prohibition has been faithfully observed by Muhammadans. There are, so far as I know, but few paintings of the prophet in existence which can boast a moderate antiquity, and if Christian art provides an analogy it would have been the prophet himself that would have formed the subject of every devout painter. Love of colour and design has found an outlet in the direction indicated in the last tradition quoted.

It is believed by Muslims that God has created a remedy for every disease. Probably a primitive view of the healing art is that which limits the patient to three prescriptions—cupping, purging, and cauterizing. Ibn 'Abbās puts it thus: 'Cures are wrought

[1] One is irresistibly reminded in this hadith of the constant allusion in the Talmud to the difference between the earthly artist and the heavenly designer. Cf. *Berakoth* 10a and *Megilla* 14a, where the word is the same (*ṣūr*).

by three things: letting blood, drinking honey, and cautery; the latter I forbid my people.' On the other hand, two hadith mention the occasions on which the prophet cauterized the wounds of his followers.

Bukhārī's *Kitābu-l-Tibb*[1] contains two interesting hadith:

(*a*) 'Āisha is the speaker: 'The prophet used to say to the sick, "Bismillahi![2] The soil of our land with the spittle of some of us will cure our sick."'

(*b*) 'The apostle of God used to say in a magical formula (*fi-l-ruqyati*)[2]: "Bismillahi! the soil of our land with the spittle of some of us will cure our sick by the permission of our Lord."'

Significant and interesting is the hadith which registers the protest of those who feel that the 'tradition of the fathers' is becoming a burden and is without the authority it claims. 'Abd Allah b. Mas'ūd said: 'God has cursed women who tattoo and those who seek to be tattooed, those who pluck out hair,[3] and those who make openings in their front teeth by way of coquetry, who alter what God has created.' A woman came to him and said: 'I have been told that you have cursed such and such women.' He replied: 'What can I do but curse those whom the apostle of God has cursed and those who are cursed in God's

[1] Krehl, iv, p. 63.

[2] I think that Houdas (iv, p. 79) has missed the point that the *Bismillah* in both these traditions is the *ruqya*. See Lane, *ME*, p. 258, and Zwemer (*op. cit.*, p. 166).

[3] Cf. the lines:

wa)-(rā'i'atin lammā allamat bi)-(mafriqī
talaqqaituhā khaufa-l-faḍīḥati bil-qaṭfi
(fa)-qālat 'alā ḍu'fī qawīta wa-innanī
ṭali'atu jaishin saufa ya'tīka min khalfī.

book?' She said: 'But I have read what lies between the two tablets, and have not found a trace of what you adduce.' He answered: 'If you had read it you would have found it. Have you not read, "What the prophet has brought you receive; and what he has forbidden you avoid?"' (Sur. lix. 7.) 'Yes, certainly,' said she. 'Then verily he has forbidden this,' was Ibn Mas'ūd's rejoinder.

It will be seen that the significance of this tradition lies in the underlying argument. The test 'What the prophet has brought you' does not only refer to the Quranic injunction and revelation: it applies also to what the prophet said or was reported to have said on some occasion when he was admittedly not repeating the message of his heavenly visitant.

VI

BORROWING FROM CHRISTIAN DOCUMENTS AND TRADITION

Muslims accuse one another of slavishly imitating Christians.—Imitation of miracles of Christ; of sayings; of parables.—Ascetics and Monks.—Logia of Jesus.

WITHIN a few years of the prophet's death the Muslims were masters of Syria, Mesopotamia and Egypt, lands inhabited by nations which from a remote antiquity possessed traditions of civilization and culture. As we have seen, Islam at this time was undeveloped both as regards theory and practice, and we should *a priori* expect to see in the traditional literature some traces of that borrowing from Judaism and Christianity with which Muhammad in the pages of the Quran has long familiarized us. Nor is this expectation unrealized; for we find that many of the same speculations agitated the minds of Muhammadan theologians and thinkers before a rigid orthodoxy was enforced by the power of the sword as find expression in the writings of Christian theologians of that time.

The broad tolerance of the early Umayyads promoted the freest intercourse between their followers and the Christians of their capital. We find Akhtal, a Christian, the official court poet, and John of Damascus and his father high in the councils of the caliph. So genial were the relations between Muslims and Christians that we find the latter moving unhindered with the cross openly displayed on their breasts within the mosques of their Muslim friends. In such an atmosphere of freedom and tolerance theological discussions must have abounded. To this unhindered intercourse of Muslim and Christian theologians is due the similarity between many of the dogmas of Islam and Christianity. This, of course, was not the only channel through which Christian thought percolated to the Islamic mind; but it was one of the earliest, and one which has left a permanent mark on the thought and literature of Islam.[1]

Down to Abbasid times there was evidently opportunity for the exchange of ideas, as the *Risāla* of Al Kindī, written in the reign of Al Ma'mūn, proves. The hadith literature preserves a very large number of examples of this borrowing, ranging from the earliest and best-known doctrines of Islam, which were taken over from Jews and Christians, and are already incorporated in the Quran, to those sayings attributed to the prophet which betray a knowledge of Christian writings. Muslim theologians were not content to borrow the sayings of their predecessors in the counsels of God: they borrowed also events from the life of Jesus, attributing them to their own prophet. Muhammad himself constantly insisted that he was not sent to work miracles. His miracle for all time was the

[1] The great tolerance displayed towards Jews and Christians during the first centuries is well illustrated in the saying reported by Abū Huraira (Bukhārī): The People of the Book used to read the Tora in Hebrew and expound it in Arabic to the people of Islām. The apostle of God said: 'Do not believe the people of the book and do not disbelieve them, but say, "We believe in God and what he has revealed to us."'

Quran. This is the opinion held by the authors of the oldest hadith: the chapter *Faḍāilu-l-sayyidi-l-mursalīn* does not contain a single miracle of Muhammad's: on the contrary, there is the express statement of Abū Huraira that whereas the former prophets were given signs to induce the people to believe, Muhammad was given only the Quran, which nevertheless might secure him more followers than all that were before him. Naturally people who were familiar with many of the noblest writings of all time denied the claim of Muslims to possess a book of surpassing literary merit; and the polemical literature of the time abounds in taunts that Muhammad could not have been a prophet because, unlike the Messiah and the earlier prophets of Israel, he worked no miracles.

It is interesting to notice that apparently the only miracles said to have been performed by Muhammad and known to Al Kindī are: the wolf and ox that spoke; the tree that moved towards the prophet; the shoulder of goat's flesh, poisoned by Zainab bint Ḥārith the Jewess, which called out that it was poisoned; and the miraculous production of water. Some, this writer says, the Aṣḥābu-l-Akhbār reject altogether, while others are from reporters branded *ḍaʿīf*.[1] Al Kindī's testimony to enlightened opinion on these miracles is worthy of note, because he wrote some years before Al Bukhārī's collection was made, and he expressly refers (p. 60) to the traditions in terms which imply that they were not written.

Muhammadan apologists could not afford to allow their apostle to labour under the disadvantage appa-

[1] He calls them *Akhbārun bāridatun wa-kharāfātu ʿajāiz*, 'witless fables and old wives' tales'.

rent when his everyday mundane life was compared with the mighty works of Christ, which seem to have been believed without question. And thus the curious and interesting fact is that the later picture of Muhammad approximates in tradition ever more closely to that of the Jesus of the gospels. No biographer, either ancient or modern, has succeeded in giving his readers an entirely satisfactory appreciation of the baffling personality of the great prophet of Arabia. His loyalty and treachery, abstinence and debauchery, wisdom and ignorance, mediocrity and inspiration, demand the pen of a Boswell.

The most prejudiced among his followers or his enemies could hardly trace in the authentic record of Muhammad's life the lineaments of the Prince of Peace. Yet this is what a certain group of traditionists and theologians have constructed. Weary of hearing of the acts of love and mercy, of supernatural power and forgiveness of 'Īsā b. Maryam, they have made a Muhammad after his likeness. Not content with the picture of a courteous, kindly, and able man, famed as the possessor of all human virtues, the idol of his race, if he was to compete with the Messiah they must represent him as a worker of miracles. There is an unmistakable reference to the slavish imitation of Christians in the plaint put into the prophet's mouth, 'Verily you would follow the paths (*sunan*) of those who were before you foot by foot and inch by inch so that if they went down a lizard's hole you would follow them!' 'Do you mean the Jews and Christians?' said they. 'And who else?' he answered.

The most obvious imitation of the New Testament miracles is that based on the 'feeding of the five thousand' (John ii. 1–11). A large number of variants are extant. The version cited below is perhaps the most interesting: Anas said: 'Abū Ṭalḥa said to Umm Sulaim, "The voice of the apostle of God sounded to me weak: I know he is hungry. Have you anything to eat?" "Yes," said she, and bringing out some barley loaves she wrapped them in her veil. Then she put them in my hand, and wound the rest of the veil round my head, and sent me to the apostle of God. I brought them to him in the mosque where he was with the people. I saluted them, and the apostle of God said to me, "Did Abū Ṭalḥa send you with food?" "Yes," said I. The apostle said to those who were with him, "Arise." And he went off to Abū Ṭalḥa's house, while I led the way and told Abū Ṭalḥa, who cried, "O Umm Sulaim, the apostle of God has come with a company and we have nothing to give them to eat!" She answered: "God and his apostle know best!" So Abū Ṭalḥa went forth to meet the apostle, and they came together. He said: "Produce what you have, Umm Sulaim," and she brought that bread, and the apostle ordered it to be broken, and Umm Sulaim squeezed a butter skin to season it. Then the apostle said grace. "Call ten men," said he; and they called them, and they ate and were well filled and went out. Then he said the same words again, and all the people ate and were well filled, and they were in number seventy or eighty men.'[1]

Sometimes this miracle takes the form of miraculously supplying water in the desert for a large number of men; and the detail is added that water ran from the prophet's fingers in order to enable the people to

[1] *Mishkāt*, p. 529.

perform *wuḍu*. Most of these miracles will be found in the chapter Mu'jizāt of the *Mishkāt*.

Again, it is interesting to compare the acts of healing performed by the prophet with those recorded in the New Testament. Yazīd b. Abū 'Ubaid says: 'I saw the mark of a wound on Salma's leg, and I said, "O Abū Muslim, what is this wound?" He answered, "It is a wound I received on the day of Khaibar, when it was said Salma is smitten to death. And I came to the prophet, who blew on the wound three times, and I have not felt it from that day to this."' Cf. Mark vii. 33.

There is a close parallel to the man possessed with an unclean spirit in the story of the woman with the demoniac son (*bihi jinnatun*). The prophet takes hold of him by the nostril, crying, 'Come forth, for I am Muhammad the apostle of God.'[1]

The Companions of the prophet, like the apostles of the New Testament, enjoy some of the special privileges of their master: thus two of them were lighted on their homeward way at nightfall by a staff;[2] another foretells his death; and Abū Bakr's food is miraculously increased.[3] The very clothes of Muhammad and his shorn hair have virtue to heal the sick and to

[1] *Op. cit.*, p. 532. The story, fathered on Ibn 'Abbās, of the boy possessed by unclean spirits who vomited, at the apostle's touch, a thing like a black puppy, is reminiscent of the Syriac *Acta Martyrum* rather than the Gospels.

[2] This recalls somewhat similar stories of the greater Rabbis. It is hardly possible, without a systematic investigation of the hadith literature and the Talmud, to determine whether the borrowing has been from Judaism or Christianity. This is a subject to which I shall recur elsewhere.

[3] *Op. cit.*, pp. 536 f.

cure those under the power of the evil eye. Cf. Acts xix. 12.

Controversy with Christians on the rival merits of Jesus and Muhammad may fairly be regarded as the origin of the pretended miracles, flatly contradicting the plain statement of the great Arabian and those of many of his immediate followers that he was not sent with power to work miracles. Whether the object of the inventors was to elevate their prophet to a position equal to that held by Jesus in the estimation of His servants, or whether it was to furnish themselves and their pupils with a messenger of God who satisfied a natural craving of the human heart for a visible manifestation of divine power, it is not our purpose to determine. There are good reasons for believing that deliberate imitation was resorted to for the reasons already given, and because the aṣḥābu-l-hadith did not stop at ascribing the works of Christ to their prophet. His words and those of his apostles are freely drawn on and put into the mouth of Muhammad.[1]

It is unnecessary to do more than set out some of the sayings of Jesus which have been attributed to Muhammad, and leave them to speak for themselves.

1. 'Abd Allāh b. 'Umar. A man came to the prophet and said: 'O apostle of God, how often are we to forgive a servant?' He remained silent. Then

[1] Muhammadan critics quite frankly draw a clear line between hadith of a legal and an edifying nature. They confess that where a pious motive underlies a tradition there is not the same necessity for scrutinizing the isnad. Thus Al Nawawī says of a hadith of this kind, 'it is weak, but one is delighted by it'; and Aḥmad says that he deals gently with the genealogy of traditions concerning virtuous behaviour.

the man repeated the question three times, and finally he answered, 'Forgive him seventy times every day.' Cf. Matt. xviii. 21.

2. Nu'mān b. Bashīr. The apostle of God said: 'Believers in their mutual compassion, love, and kindness are like the body. When it aileth in a member it summons all the body to it in sleeplessness and fever (*muttafaq 'alaihi*).' Another version from the same guarantor is: Believers are as one man. If a man's eye pains him his whole body suffers, and if his head pains him he suffers everywhere (Muslim). Cf. 1 Cor. xii. 13–26 and Eph. iv. 16.

3. Abū Mūsā. The relation of believer to believer is as a building. One part strengthens another. Then (by way of illustration) he interlaced his fingers. Cf. Eph. ii. 21.

4. Ibn Mas'ūd. None will enter hell who has in his heart faith of the weight of a grain of mustard seed; nor shall any one enter heaven who has in his heart pride of the weight of a grain of mustard seed. Cf. Matt. xvii. 20.

5. Anas: God does not deprive a believer of his reward in the world to come for a good deed, though he has been recompensed on earth; but an unbeliever is nourished in this world for the good deeds he has done for God, so that when he passes to the next world he has no good deed for which he can be rewarded. Cf. Matt. vi. 1–2.

6. Abū Huraira: There will go forth in the end of time men who will deceive the world in religion, they will appear to men clad in sheep skins for softness, their tongues will be sweeter than sugar, and their hearts are the hearts of wolves. God will say: 'Is it

with me ye are careless, or against me ye are bold? I swear by myself I will send against those men a punishment which will leave the wise man with understanding of the enigma.'

7. Abū Huraira: Blessed is he who hath seen me, and sevenfold blessed is he who hath not seen me and yet hath believed in me. Cf. John xx. 29.

Doubtless a search through the Six Books would reveal a large addition to the instances I have cited. To them may be added the examples quoted by Goldziher,[1] which I have refrained from reproducing. The New Testament references are: Matt. v. 3; vii. 5 and 6; ix. 2–7; x. 16; xvi. 24; and xxii. 21.

The chapter on the Excellence of the Poor[2] contains a selection of sayings which amply illustrate the extent to which the 'other-worldliness' of the New Testament influenced some of the thinkers of Islam. Riches are in themselves evil: they are the portion in this life of those who will perish in the next: the poor will enter paradise five hundred years before the rich: the world is a prison to the believer: all of which suggest an affinity in attitude and aspiration to the teaching of sections of the New Testament.

Of the parables of Jesus which have been transferred to Muhammad we may cite the following:

1. The Labourers in the Vineyard. Matt. xx. 1–16. Ibn 'Umar. Your age compared with the age of the peoples who were before you is as the time between afternoon prayer and sunset. You, the Jews, and the Christians, may be compared unto a man who employed labourers, saying, 'Who will work for me till noon for a qīrāṭ?' The Jews worked till noon for a qīrāṭ.

[1] *Op. cit.*, pp. 384 ff.

[2] *Mishkāt*, pp. 438 ff.

Then he said: 'Who will work for me from noon till afternoon prayer for a qīrāṭ?' The Christians did so. Then he said: 'Who will work for me from afternoon prayer to sunset for two qīrāt?' Ye are the latter. Have ye not a double reward? And the Jews and Christians were angry, and said: 'We have worked more and received less.' God said: 'Have I wronged you of your due?' They said, 'No.' He said: 'It is my grace. I give to whom I will.' (Bukhārī's versions, see Ijāra and Tauḥīd, differ considerably.)

2. The Wedding Guests. Matt. xxii. 1–10. Jābir. Angels visited the prophet while he was asleep, and said to one another: 'There is a parable of this friend of yours, so propound a parable to him.' But some said, 'He sleeps'; others, 'His eye sleeps but his heart is awake.' So they said: 'He is like unto a man who built a house and made therein a feast, and sent forth one to bid men come. And those who accepted the invitation of the summoner entered the house and ate of the feast, and those who refused neither entered nor ate.' They said: 'Explain it to him so that he may understand.' Some said, 'He sleeps'; others, 'His eye sleeps but his heart is awake.' So they explained: the house is paradise, the summoner Muhammad; for he who obeys Muhammad obeys God, and whosoever disobeys Muhammad disobeys God, Muhammad being the dividing difference (*farq*) between men' (Bukhārī).

3. The Sower. Matt. xiii. 3–12. Abū Mūsā. 'The guidance and knowledge wherewith God has sent me is like unto abundant rain that falleth on earth, of which the good part receives the water and brings forth grass and herbage manifold. And part is high ground that retains the water wherewith God profits

men in that they drink, water their beasts, and sow their seed. And some of the rain falls on another part which is flat ground, neither retaining the water nor bringing forth grass. The two first are like unto a man who understands God's religion and the message God entrusted to me profits him, and he understands and teaches it. And the last is like unto the man who does not honour nor receive God's guidance with which I was sent.'

Many of the traditions quoted above found their way into the canonical collections through the same channel as the moral and didactic sayings current among the Arabs themselves, or among the Jews and other nations whose culture was so freely drawn on in the formative period of the history of Islam. These traditions circulated first as a *ḥādīth mauqūfa*[1] (i. e. traceable only to a Companion or Follower). To gain a respectful hearing they required the stamp of the prophet himself. A missing name or two was all that was needed to make the chain complete, and this was supplied by the pious fraud who bore a special designation *Raffāʿ*, because he made the hadith *marfuʿ*[1] carried back to the prophet himself.

Nothing could be further removed from the point of view of the ordinary Arab of the Jāhiliyya or of Islam than asceticism, as the formidable array of hadith condemning it in all its forms clearly testify. Of these one example must suffice.

Anas: 'Three men came to the prophet's wives questioning them about his devotion (*ʿibāda*). When they were told they were for despising slightly his

[1] See Glossary.

devotion, saying, "Where do we come short of the prophet? And God has pardoned his sins past and future." One of them said: "As for me I will ever pray by night." The second said: "I will ever fast by day and not break by fast." The third: "I will turn aside from women and never marry." Then the prophet came to them, and said: "Are ye they who speak thus? Verily I am the most God-fearing and pious among you, yet I fast and break my fast. I pray and sleep; I marry women. And he who turns away from my *sunna* is none of mine."'

A certain tendency to asceticism was always latent in Islam from the days when Muhammad first proclaimed the judgement of God one day to be pronounced against sinners, and the punishments of hell for those who lived without God in the world. Indeed reflections and meditations on the transitoriness of human life and a Day of Reckoning to come are not unknown in the poetry of the pre-Islamic period. But they are not of native origin: they are to be ascribed to the influence of Christian monks and communities, and also to Jewish monotheists scattered over Arabia.

The amazing successes of the Caliphs' armies, bringing in their train an influx of wealth which, even at the present day would be thought stupendous, could not but turn men's thoughts and ambitions towards worldly things. This tendency to covetousness and worldliness was apparent to, and condemned by, the prophet, 'You desire the passing wealth of this world,' he exclaims, 'but God desires the next world' (Sur. viii. 68). Ibn Sa'd furnishes us with details of the colossal fortunes bequeathed to their heirs by those reputed the holiest among the prophet's associates: thus Ṭalḥa

b. 'Ubaid Allah is said to have died leaving a hundred leather sacks each containing three qīnṭārs of ingots.[1] The early hadith are full of stories of the grinding poverty and want of the early Muhammadans. Ṭalḥa's father relates that when he and his friends complained to the prophet of their hunger they each took a stone from their bellies, and the prophet took two from his.[2] It is not surprising if a people which in a generation had passed from the extreme of indigence to the height of wealth and luxury should show active dislike of those who taught the vanity of riches. Yet even so among a minority the ideal of *Weltverneinung* lived on.

There was always a strife between those who fought for the gain of this world and those who strove *'ala-l-ākhira*. Abu Sa'īd Al Khudrī is the mouthpiece of those who took the middle view that wealth in itself is harmless if it does not lead to avarice and extravagant display.[3] This was the view of the ordinary Muslim, who stood midway between the Ascetic and the Plutocrat.

Probably the reason why asceticism provoked so much opposition and gave rise to so many hadith in its condemnation was that, like the doctrine of man's free will, it was recognized that its immediate origin was Christian. Many of the hadith directed against asceticism, like 'There is no monasticism in Islam—

[1] Eine schwere Ladung für das Paradies! Goldziher, *Vorlesungen*, p. 141.

[2] There are frequent references in hadith to the custom of tying stones on the belly to still the craving for food, and to enable men to walk upright. *Mishkāt*, p. 440. Hunger was the driving force behind the Arab migration. See Caetani, *Annali*, ii, *passim*.

[3] *Mishkāt*, p. 431.

the monasticism (*rahbāniyya*) of my community is the Jihād', bear the obvious stamp of anti-Christian polemic.[1] The Christian monks had long been settled in Arabia. Muhammad in the Quran (9. 113 and 66. 5) speaks of them not unfavourably. And when the conquest and occupation of Syria, Egypt, and Mesopotamia brought Muhammadans into daily intercourse with monks and nuns, those to whom a life of prayer and meditation and poverty appealed were not slow to copy closely the practices of their Christian neighbours. These early Ṣūfīs drew from the New Testament the parables and sayings of Jesus which seemed to sanction and commend the ascetic life; and very early in their history a work full of thinly-disguised extracts from the Christians' bible was circulated. Margoliouth writes of Abū 'Abd Allah al Ḥārith b. Asad al Muḥāsibī (d. 243 A.H.):

'It is to be noticed that these sermons show evident traces of the use of the Gospel, as indeed the work on the "Observation of God's Claims" commences with a repetition of the Parable of the Sower without distinct mention of its source. The Keuprülü treatise, which is against hypocrisy, might be said to be an expansion of the doctrines of the Sermon on the Mount: and to the phraseology of the Gospels there seem to be some clear allusions: these may be due to infiltration or to actual study of the Gospels on the author's part.'[2]

An extremely interesting collection of *Logia et*

[1] 'In the early part of the third century it appears that the Muslim ascetic was not easily distinguished from the Christian; and, indeed, they had much in common.'—Margoliouth, *Early Development*, p. 141.

[2] *Transactions of the Third International Congress for the History of Religions*, i, p. 292, Oxford, 1908.

Agrapha attributed to Christ by Muhammadan writers was made by Professor Asin,[1] who explains their origin thus:

'Slowly and by degrees monasticism, an institution execrated by Muhammad,[2] was evolved in the succeeding centuries, and was developed to such a point that it lacked none of the essentials of Christian monasticism. . . . Now from what seed could this mystical tree of monastic perfection grow in the arid soil of Muhammadanism? No other source can be imagined than Christian monasticism, which was well known to the Muslims, and not unknown to the pre-Islamic Arabs. . . . Therefore it is not to be wondered at if, after the Christian institution of monasticism began to put forth roots among the Muslims, the example of Christian monks was imitated by the Muslims themselves, and they at once endeavoured as far as possible to destroy the anti-monastic lineaments, so to speak, of Muhammad, both by forging traditions in which the words and deeds of Jesus are attributed to Muhammad, and by publishing the precepts and precedents, authentic or apocryphal, of Jesus, so that His authority might lend strength to their ascetic innovations. . . . Without

[1] *Logia et Agrapha Domini Jesu apud Moslemicos scriptores, asceticos praesertim, usitata* . . . Michael Asin et Palacios (*Patrologia Orientalis*, Tome xiii, Fasc. 3, Paris (n. d.), p. 338).

[2] It may be doubted whether this statement is altogether justifiable. 'Know ye that this world's life is only a sport and pastime and show and a cause of vainglory among you' (Sur. 57, 19), would suggest the advisability of withdrawing from the affairs of this world. Ver. 27, 'We put into the hearts of those who followed him (Jesus) kindness and compassion: but as to the monastic life (*rahbāniyya*) they invented it themselves' (cf. Rodwell, 9. 31), is hardly an execration. But possibly Dr. Asin is referring to some of the hadith quoted above.

doubt the *Logia* ascribed to Jesus by Muslim writers are connected with a settled (*certa*) Christian tradition among the Oriental churches, orthodox or heterodox, before the seventh century A. D. Now I do not say that this tradition is entirely free from error: indeed it has been corrupted by their traditionists; yet not intentionally, but rather from the accidents inseparable from all oral tradition. The simple choice of words, the ingenuous character of the narrative, full as it is of anachronisms, both as to time and place, point to the vehicle of transmission being not written but oral tradition handed on in the first place by the common people before it was recorded by theologians.'

The examples given below, quoted from more than a hundred collected by Asin, are all taken from Al Ghazālī's great work the *Iḥyāu 'Ulūmi-l-Dīn*. Ghazālī lived in the eleventh and twelfth centuries, though the traditions, for the most part, are demonstrably centuries older.

1. Jesus said, 'Do not hang pearls on the necks of swine. Verily wisdom is better than pearls, and he who despises it is worse than swine.' Cf. Matt. vii. 6. Al Ghazālī, *Ih.* I. 43. 4.

2. It is related that God revealed to Jesus: 'If you worship me with the worship of the dwellers in heaven and earth and have not love in God[1] and hatred in God, that will not profit thee aught.' *Ih.* II. 110. 15. The same in a somewhat different form is ascribed in 110. 6 to 'Abd Allah b. Umar. 'By God, though I fast all day without sustenance and rise spending the night in prayer and spend my wealth purse by purse

[1] For the Christian genesis of the expression *fi-llah* and *billah* in tradition, see *MS*, ii, p. 392.

in the way of God, and when I die there is no love in my heart towards the people who obey God, nor hatred to those who disobey Him that will not profit me aught.' Cf. 1 Cor. xiii. 1–3.

3. It is related that the devil appeared to 'Īsā b. Maryam, and said: 'Say, "There is no God but the God."' He replied, 'The saying is true, but I will not say it with your voice because it has ambiguity beneath the good.' A cryptic synopsis of Matt. iv. 3–10: *Ih.* III. 23. 19.

4. Jesus said: 'Blessed is he who leaves present desire for a promise not present which he does not see.' *Ih.* III. 48. 8: cf. John xii. 25.

5. The Messiah passed by a company of Jews, who cursed Him, but He blessed them. It was said to Him: 'They speak Thee evil and Thou speakest them well!' He answered: 'Every one spends of that which he hath.' *Ih.* III. 123. 19: cf. Matt. xii. 34, 35 and Luke vi. 8 and 45.

6. It was said to Jesus: 'Teach us one precept ('ilm) for keeping which God will love us.' He answered: 'Hate the world and God will love you.' *Ih.* III. 141. 10: cf. John xii. 25; xv. 18, 19. Practically the same hadith is put in the mouth of the prophet by Tirmidhī and Ibn Māja on the authority of Sahal b. Sa'd. It reads thus: A man came and said: 'O Apostle of God, teach me a work the which if I accomplish God and mankind will love me.' He replied: 'Renounce the world and God will love you. Renounce what mankind possess and mankind will love you.'[1]

[1] Since I wrote this paragraph, I see that Goldziher (*Vorlesungen*, p. 188) quotes this hadith as one of the 'Forty Traditions' of Nawawī. Apparently he is incorrect in saying 'Der Spruch findet sich nicht in

7. Jesus said: 'The world is a bridge. Therefore cross it; do not dwell on it.'[1] *Ih.* III. 149. 11.

8. 'When death was mentioned in the presence of Jesus his skin used to distil blood.' *Ih.* IV. 325. 12. This remarkable tradition is evidently based on the agony in the garden described in Luke xxii. 44.

9. 'It is related that when Jesus the Son of Mary was born the devils came to Satan and said: "To-day the idols are overthrown and their heads broken." He said: "A new thing has happened. Keep in your places." So he flew unto the ends of the earth and found nothing. Then he found that Jesus had been born, and lo angels were encompassing him. And he returned unto the devils and said: "Verily a prophet was born yesterday. Never has a woman conceived or brought forth but I was present with her, except this. Therefore the idols despair of being worshipped after to-night. Nevertheless tempt the sons of men (to act) with haste and levity."' III. 26. 4. This is in keeping with the canonical tradition recorded by Bukhārī that the only child untouched at birth by Satan was Jesus.

den strengern Sammlungen und blosz aus dem Traditionswerk des Ibn Mādscha nachgewiesen', if the compiler of the *Mishkāt* is to be believed. The latter writes, 'rawāhu Al Tirmidhī wabnu Māja'.

[1] 'This appears to me to be an agraphum,' Asin. The words occur in an inscription on the great gateway of the mosque of Fathpūr-Sīkrī erected by Akbar in 1601.

VII

SOME ASPECTS OF THE PROPHET MUHAMMAD IN TRADITION

Our purpose is not to attempt to give a coherent biography of the Arabian prophet, or even to mention the principal incidents in his life. Material for this must be sought elsewhere.[1] But simply because no survey of the hadith literature, however superficial, would be complete without some account of the impression it gives of the enigmatic personality of its great hero, a few hadith are translated to supplement what has gone before, and to show particularly how, with the passing of years, the fallible, human figure of Muhammad has faded into oblivion. The gulf between the prophet who is believed to have worked the miracles mentioned on page 136 and him who spoilt the date crop of Medina by his untimely interference with established custom could not have been bridged in one or two generations.

Many of the hadith already cited will have shown the good sense, amiability, and liberality of the prophet; and the following further examples of the qualities which have ever endeared him to his followers must suffice.

Rafi' b. 'Amr al Ghaffārī: 'When I was a boy I threw stones at the Anṣār's date-palms, and so they brought me before the prophet of God. "Boy," said he, "why

[1] See especially the works of Caetani, Muir, Margoliouth, Sprenger, and others; also Ibn Sa'd and Ibn Hishām.

did you throw stones at the date-palms?" "So that I might eat dates," I said. "Don't throw stones," said he, "but eat the fallings." Then he touched his head and prayed: "O God, satisfy him with food."' 'Āisha: 'A man asked permission to see the prophet of God, who said: "Let him come in though he is of an evil tribe." When the man sat with him the prophet showed him a bright countenance and conversed agreeably with him. After he had gone 'Āisha asked: "How is it that you treated him so kindly when you had thus spoken of him?" He replied: "When have you known me immoderate in speech? The worst men in God's sight on the day of resurrection will be those whom men forsake through dread of their wickedness"' (variant: harsh speech).[1] The *Bābu-l-Muzāḥ* contains a pleasing notice of the prophet's kindness to children and his fondness of jokes and raillery, which may be further illustrated from the story of his relation to his child-wife. 'Āisha said: 'The apostle of God returned from the raid of Tabūk (variant: or Hunain). Now her booth was protected by a curtain, and when the wind blew aside the edge of the curtain 'Āisha's dolls were seen. "What are these?" asked Muhammad. "My dolls," she answered. Then he noticed among them a horse with two wings of patchwork, and was told what the object was. "A horse with two wings!" he exclaimed. "Have you not heard", she replied, "that Solomon possessed winged horses?" 'Āisha, in relating the hadith, adds: "Then he laughed so that I could see his molars."'

[1] Commentators differ as to the meaning of this last sentence. It reads rather like a protest against the autocratic bearing of the caliphs than a recommendation of courtesy towards the wicked.

But their relations were not always so easy. There are frequent references to the domestic troubles of the prophet which sometimes scandalized his followers. We read of the anger of Abū Bakr when his daughter dared to scold the prophet in a voice that could be heard without. Exclaiming, 'I will not hear thee lift thy voice against the apostle of God,' he seized hold of her to slap her face. But the prophet restrained him so that he went out in anger. When he had gone the prophet said, 'You see how I have delivered you from the man.'[1] Abū Bakr remained unreconciled for some days. Then he called and found the pair at peace, and said, 'Include me in your peace as you included me in your quarrel!' The prophet answered, 'We do! we do!' Another occasion of strife is connected with the dispute between Muhammad and his wives which has found its way into the Quran (Sur. 33. 51). Its guarantor is Jābir: Abū Bakr came asking to see the apostle of God, and found people who had been refused admittance sitting at his door. Abū Bakr was allowed to enter, and was followed subsequently by 'Umar. They found the prophet sitting, surrounded by his wives, gloomy and silent. 'Umar said: 'I must say something to make the prophet laugh'; so he began: 'O apostle of God, if I see Bint Khārija asking me for money then I get up and throttle her!' The apostle of God said: 'These women about me, as you see, are asking for money.' So Abū Bakr got up and throttled 'Āisha, and 'Umar treated Ḥafṣa similarly, saying: 'Will you ask the apostle of God for what he does not possess?' They said: 'By God, we never ask him for anything he does not possess!' Then he sepa-

[1] The commentators suppose the remark to be a jest.

rated himself from them for a month (variant: or twenty-nine days), when this revelation descended: 'O prophet, say to thy wives, if ye desire this present life and its braveries, come then I will provide for you and dismiss you with an honourable dismissal. But if ye desire God and his apostle and a home in the next life, then truly hath God prepared for those of you who are virtuous a great reward.'[1] He told 'Āisha of this first, saying: 'I wish to lay a matter before you in the which I desire that you do not decide until you shall have consulted your parents.' When she inquired what it was he recited the revelation to her. She responded: 'Is it about you that I am to consult my parents? Nay, but I choose God and his apostle and the home in the next life. I ask you, however, not to inform any of your other wives of what I have said.' His answer was, 'If any of them ask me I shall tell them, for God has not sent me to cause chagrin and sin, but to teach and to make (righteousness) easy.'

Probably nothing is more illustrative of the prophet's greatness both among his contemporaries and with posterity than the fact that his reputation could survive the publication of the following story by his wife 'Āisha: 'I was jealous of the women who gave themselves to the apostle of God, and said, "Does a woman give herself?" Then when God revealed: "Thou mayest decline for the present whom thou wilt of them, and thou mayest take to thy bed her whom thou wilt, and whomsoever thou shalt long for of those thou shalt have before neglected; and this shall not be

[1] Sur. 33. 28–9. The translation is Rodwell's. The text has only the opening and the final words of the verses. Cf. Muir, p. 304, where the passage is connected with the scandal that gathered round 'Āisha.

a crime in thee."[1] I said, "I see your Lord does nothing but hasten to fulfil your desire!"'[2] In this context we may include the significant tradition of Anas recorded by Al Nasā'ī, 'After women nothing was dearer to the apostle of God than horses.'[3]

In a hadith of Umm Salma the prophet freely admits his fallibility: 'I am only mortal, and when you come disputing before me perhaps some of you are more eloquent in argument than others, and I give judgement according to what I hear. But whoso receives judgement in this way to the detriment of his brother's rights let him not take it, for if he does I have reserved a place in hell for him.'

But the clearest possible recognition of Muhammad's ignorance of everyday matters is to be found in the story of his interference with the process of fertilizing date-palms. Rāfi' b. Khadīj: 'The prophet of God came to Medina when they were fecundating the date-

[1] v. 51.

[2] It must be counted unto the traditionists for righteousness that this and the many other hadith so damaging to the prophet's reputation were not expunged from the canonical collections. It would seem that the prophet's character among the faithful was above criticism; otherwise it is difficult to see how such traditions could have been tolerated in a community which claimed to have received a revelation from God.

[3] The contradictory nature of some of the hadith is well illustrated by the following sayings which claim to reflect the prophet's preference in the matter of horses:

(*a*) Abū Qutāda. The best horses are black with white foreheads and white upper lip. Then a black horse with a white forehead and three white legs; then a bay with these markings.

(*b*) Abū Wahab. A bay with a white forehead and white legs is the best.

(*c*) Ibn 'Abbās. Prosperity goes with the sorrel.

palms,[1] and asked what was being done. It was replied that this was custom. "Perhaps it would be better if you did not do it," said he. So they left the trees as they were and the crop was deficient. When the people told him of this, he said: "I am only mortal. If I give you an order in the domain of your religion then receive it; but if I give you an order from my own opinion (*rai*) then am I but mortal."'

There is also preserved the story of Muhammad's unsuccessful negotiations with a Jew. The story comes from 'Āisha: 'The prophet wore two thick *Qiṭrī*[2] garments, so that when he sat down perspiring he found them oppressive. Now clothes had come from Syria to a certain Jew, so I said: "If you were to send to him and buy (sc. on credit) two garments you would be more at ease." So he sent, and the fellow said: "I know what you want: you only want to go off with my money!" The apostle of God said: "He lies: for he knows that I am the most God-fearing and punctilious in money matters of all men." In another hadith she repeats: "If you wish to cleave to me then be satisfied with the portion of a horseman in this world, and beware of sitting with the rich, nor think a garment shabby until it has been patched."'[3] Though the last is probably not a genuine hadith it

[1] See Margoliouth and Muir *in loc.*; and Burton, *Pilgrimage*, p. 403, for a description of the process.

[2] The commentator explains this as 'a kind of Yaman garment'. The *Nihaya* says it is a garment dyed red with rough coarse fringes, and offers another explanation to the effect that it comes from Baḥrain.

[3] This tradition bears the warning: Al Tirmidhī relates it, and says, 'This is a *gharīb* hadith. We only know it from the hadith of Ṣāliḥ b. Ḥassān. Muhammad b. Isma'īl (i.e. Al Bukhārī) says the latter is *munkiru-l-hadith*.' See Glossary.

points rightly to the poverty and privation in which the prophet and his friends lived, to which allusion has already been made on p. 144. The same authority (in Bukhārī) tells us that the prophet's family did not eat barley bread for two consecutive days during the whole of his life, a statement which is strengthened by Anas, who says that he went to the prophet with some barley bread and rancid dripping, and found that he had pawned his coat-of-mail to a Jew in Medina in exchange for barley for his family. 'Never did there remain overnight in the family of Muhammad a measure of corn or grain though he had nine wives.'

The various currents in Christian tradition, with which theologians are all familiar, represented by the Synoptic, the Apocryphal, and the Apocalyptic school, all have their counterpart in traditions which gather round the person of the founder of Islam.

Some examples of the first have already been given, while to the second belong the stories of Muhammad's miracles: the sun standing still, the splitting of the moon, and others which have already been mentioned. In the Apocalyptic hadith Muhammad stands out as the prophet of the end and consummation of all things, and as the powerful intercessor for his people with God. The following long hadith vouched for by Abū Huraira contains many of the prevailing ideas on these subjects: 'The Hour will not come till there is a fierce battle between two great forces both professing Islam; and until nearly thirty lying Dajjāls (antichrists) have been sent, each pretending that he is the apostle of God; until knowledge has been taken away and there are numerous earthquakes, till rebellions occur and commotions are frequent; till wealth be multiplied and abundant, and the wealthy will trouble him who receives alms and beg him to accept it, and it will be declined, for none need it; till men display arrogance in building, and one will pass by a man's grave and say "Would that I were in his place!" till the sun rises in the west, and all men seeing it will believe. Then will none profit by faith who has not believed aforetime and acquired virtue by faith. And the Hour will come when men have spread out their garment between them and have not agreed on a price nor folded it up; when a man shall have taken away the milk of his camel and not have drunk it; when a man shall be plaistering his cistern and have put no water in it; while a man is lifting food to his mouth and before he can eat it.' A characteristic difference between these Apocalyptic hadith and the literature as a whole is their great length. The tradition which records men's need of an intercessor on the day of resurrection and the refusal of the office successively by Adam, Noah, Abraham, Moses, and Jesus, and the triumphant intercession of Muhammad for all Muslims, contains upwards of three hundred words exclusive of the isnād. The average length of hadith on all the topics dealt with in the literature I should estimate at fifty words only.

The eschatology of the traditions of Islam—the slaying of the antichrist, the descent of Jesus son of Mary from heaven to usher in a reign of peace, prosperity, and goodness—need not be discussed here. A tradition, hardly in accord with the general content of eschatological speculation, which seems to be deeply rooted in the Muslim mind is that of 'Abd Allah b. 'Umar, which the compiler of the *Mishkāt* says is recorded by Ibn Al Jauzī in the *Kitābu-l-Wifā*: 'Jesus son of Mary will descend to the earth, marry, and beget children. He will stay on the earth forty-five years, and then die and be buried in my grave. He and I shall arise in one grave between Abū Bakr and 'Umar.'[1]

One of the most interesting subjects in Muhammadan apocalyptic is the Mi'rāj, or nocturnal journey of Muhammad to the heavenly mansions. On this incident, which is referred to in an obscure passage of the Quran (Sur. 17. 1), the reader may consult the interesting study of the learned Spanish Arabist Asin.[2] No more striking example of growth and development within the field of hadith has yet been adduced. From the story of the prophet's nocturnal journey in which he saw as in a vision the punishments of the wicked, the joys of Muslims and the felicity of martyrs, and finally Abraham, Moses, and Jesus awaiting him beneath the throne of God, there has grown up a large and extensive literature with which, in its latest form, the Occident has long been familiar in the pages of Dante Alighieri.[3]

[1] Burton, *Pilgrimage*, pp. 325 ff. 'It is popularly asserted that in the *Hujra* there is now spare place for only a single grave, reserved for 'Īsā bin Maryam after his second coming.'

[2] *La Escatología Musulmana en la Divina Comedia*, Madrid, 1919, and see my review in *Theology*, i, pp. 315–16.

[3] *Kanzu-l-'Ummāl*, Cairo, 1312, vii. 248, no. 2835, and 280, no. 3089.

APPENDIX A

THE CALIPHATE IN TRADITION

IN the following pages I have given some of the opinions of Muslim doctors on the subject of the caliphate. The subject is of greater importance in the political work of the immediate future than almost any other question in view of the fact that within the last two generations several millions of our fellow-subjects in India have prayed for the Sultan of Turkey in the Khuṭba; and it is becoming increasingly important that the place and office of the caliphate should be clearly understood in the West.

The extracts which I have made from Muslim writers will serve to show how foolish and mistaken it is for European writers to compare the caliphate with the papacy. In the sense that the learned and charming writer the Right Honourable Ameer Ali writes[1] it is of course true, but the very clear distinction between political and religious allegiance so familiar in Western states is flatly contradicted by the Muslim theory of the caliphate.

The clearest and most scholarly exposition of the caliphate is to be found in the *Muqaddima* of Ibn Khaldūn, of which following is a free translation.

The Caliph is the representative of the giver of the religious law (*Ṣāḥibu-l-sharīʿati*) in maintaining religion and governing the world. The office may be termed the Khilafate or the Imamate indifferently. When the Caliph is called Imām he is, as it were, compared with the leader, whose movements in prayer must be imitated by the whole assembly. The great Imamate is a term often used of the Caliph's office. He is called Caliph because he caliphs (i.e. succeeds or represents) the prophet; or 'the Caliph of God', or more fully,

[1] *Infra*, p. 169. I have refrained from comment.

'Caliph of the apostle of God'. Many doctors took exception to the title *khalīfatu-llāh*, and refused to admit its propriety.

The appointment of an Imām is a matter of necessity from the point of view of law founded on the Ijmā' of the Companions and Followers. Immediately on the death of the Prophet they took the oath of fealty to Abū Bakr and surrendered to him the conduct of their affairs. Succeeding centuries have followed this precedent, and such universal agreement indicates the necessity, and sanctions the setting up, of an Imām. (According to the Mu'tazilites the sole *raison d'être* of the Imām is to carry out the law: so that if the people were only righteous in their dealings there would be no need for an Imām. These views are to be attributed to their hatred of the abuse of power and position inseparable from human potentates.)

Four qualifications necessarily pertain to this office: Knowledge, Justice, Capacity (or competence), and the power to exercise the senses and limbs which reflect the activities of mind and body. A fifth condition, namely, that its holder should be a member of the tribe of the Quraish has been the subject of dispute.[1]

The first two qualities are essential because the imamate is a religious office (*manṣab dīnī*). The third, Capacity, implies courage both in internal administration and in war, statesmanship, and leadership, and a knowledge of the political situation at home and abroad. Thus there is required of him the active exercise of mind and body so that he may defend religion and fight the enemy, and thereby fulfil the commands of the law and the claims of the public weal.

The fourth condition contains an important implication. It includes the power of unrestrained action. If the Imām loses his independence through captivity or similar restraint it is as though he had lost the use of his limbs and faculties. He cannot be Imām. On the other hand, if it is only a

[1] Our author's ruler approaches the ideal, yet it is interesting to see how temporal power is, in theory at all events, indissolubly linked with the caliphate, or, as he expresses it here, the imamate.

question of the loss of some of his powers through the action of subjects who have not overtly revolted against his authority, and it is found that he acts according to the requirements of law and justice, his imamate is to be allowed. But if not, Muslims may invoke the help of one to depose him and fulfil the duties of a Caliph.

With regard to descent from the Quraish it must be admitted that the principle was accepted by the Companions on the day of Al Saqīfa. The Companions met the claim of the Medinotes to the right to elect Sa'd ibn 'Abāda by the words of the prophet, 'The Imāms are from the Quraish' (Al Āimatu min Quraishin), whereupon the Medinotes receded from their position. Moreover, there is in the Ṣaḥīḥ the authentic tradition: 'This authority shall not cease in this tribe of Quraish,' and there are many other ḥadīth to the same effect. History relates how the Quraish at home dissipated their strength in luxury and idleness, while their armies fought battles in all parts of the world, so that failure to consolidate and conserve their resources made the burden of the caliphate a task beyond their strength, and foreigners came to be invested with supreme power.

Now many doctors go so far as to deny the necessity of Quraishite birth as a qualification for an Imām, relying on the literal sense of the words of the prophet, 'Hearken and obey even if a slavering negro be set over you.' And again, 'Umar said, 'If Sālim the client of Ḥudhaifa were alive, I would have made him ruler.' The first proves nothing, for it is only a supposition; and the second rests on the opinion of only one of the Companions, and is therefore not authoritative. The great majority of Muslim doctors regard Quraishite birth as essential, and that one of that tribe must be Imām, though he be impotent to direct the affairs of the Believers. But we may refute this by pointing out that the condition of capacity cannot be fulfilled in such a case. What then was the reason for the doctrine that the Imām must be of the Quraish? Every law has a definite object, and the object of this law was not only to honour the prophet as is generally believed. It was also to ensure the safety and well-being of the Muslim people. The Quraish were formerly the noblest and bravest of the Arabs and best fitted to link together the warring factions of the Arabian peninsula. No other tribe would have been able to put an end to dissension and lead Muslims to victory. The legislator, then, declared that an Imām must be of the tribe of the Quraish because they were obviously best equipped in every respect to maintain law and order. The Quraishite domination was more or less justified under the Umayyads and Abbasids. But if we recognize the principle that the legislator is not making laws for one time and one people, we shall see that the condition of 'capacity' at once applies. Applying, then, the motive underlying the dogma that the Imām must be of the tribe of the Quraish, we say that he who guides the destinies of the Muslim peoples, like the Quraish of old, must be renowned for patriotism, influence and power: dominating his generation he must be able to command the obedience of others, and unite them in the defence of the commonwealth. When God appointed the Caliph his representative (*nāiban 'anhu*) He ordered him to seek his people's welfare and to protect them from disaster. And it is certain that He would not entrust this task to those who were impotent to fulfil it.

At this point we may note that the Shī'as' conception of the Imamate is quite different. With them the Imamate is the foundation of Islam. It cannot even be supposed that the prophet suffered the Imamate to be dependent on popular sanction. He, say they, appointed 'Alī; and though this assertion involves the branding of 'Umar and 'Uthmān as usurpers they do not stop short of this folly. To support their claim they advance certain traditions which are unknown to men learned in the *sunna* and the law. Most of them are inventions (*mauḍū'*) or come from tainted sources (*maṭ'ūn fī ṭarīqihi*); or, if genuine, are not susceptible of their corrupt interpretations. These proofs are from 'clear' and 'hidden' sources (*jalī wa khafī*). Of the first 'Who owns me as master has 'Alī as his master' is an example; of the second, we may mention their interpretation of the events at Mecca when the prophet sent Abū Bakr to inform the people of the revelation of the *sūratu-l-barāti* and afterwards sent 'Alī to read it. This shows, they argue, that 'Alī took precedence of Abū Bakr. Such are the arguments on which they rely.

The caliphate was converted into an imperial throne by the natural pressure of circumstances. In *The Ṣaḥīḥ* we read, 'God only sends a prophet when his people can defend him.' The exponent of sacred law does not care for this spirit. He prefers to lay stress on the Quranic injunctions to avoid pride and worldly display: his eyes are on the next world. Though he disapproves of imperial might he does not condemn it in its several activities, e.g. compelling respect for religion and securing the public weal. The first four Caliphs displayed a dislike towards luxury and ostentatious display of state and pomp. But this was because they had one and all been inured to the privations of a desert life. They lived on the meanest food and amid miserable conditions. The conditions prevailing in the Umayyad times made it necessary for men to rally to the reigning prince to save the country from the horrors of civil war. The later princes of this line, it must be confessed, gave themselves up to gross and sensual pleasures till the people gave the kingdom to the Abbasids. Through the impiety of some of this race the kingdom was taken from the Arabs altogether.

Yet though the caliphate became a monarchy it retained its essential characteristics for a long time. The ordinances of religion were enforced and men kept to the right paths. It was in the compelling force underlying authority that the change was made. Whereas in the past it was religion, it came to be the power of party passion (*'aṣabiyya*) and the sword. In the generation that followed the reign of Al Rashīd nothing remained of the caliphate but its name, and that only while the racial pride (*'aṣabiyya*) of the Arabs supported it. With the subjugation of the Arabs the caliphate died, and all authority was invested in the monarchy. Foreign monarchs in the East, it is true, treated the Caliphs with respect from a motive of piety, but they claimed for themselves the titles and honorifics of the monarch.

A necessary preliminary to the installation of the Caliph is the *bai'a* or oath of allegiance tendered in the name of the Muslim people. He who makes the *bai'a* recognizes the rights of the Caliph over the Muslims, and undertakes to obey all his orders whether they are agreeable to his own interests or not. He places his hand in the hand of the Caliph when pledging his faith to confirm the undertaking, just as do buyers and sellers. In fact, the word *bai'a* is derived from *bā'a*, to buy or sell; hence *bai'a* meant a mutual handtaking:[1] this is its meaning in ordinary and legal language, and, indeed, what is meant in the ḥadīth by the *bai'atu-l-nabiyyi* on the night of 'Aqaba and near the tree. So of the *bai'a* of the Caliphs and of the oath of the *bai'a*. The Caliphs used to require an oath embodying a formal declaration of assent to the compact. The *bai'a* now consists of a salutation modelled on the court of Kosroes: one must kiss the ground, the hand, foot, or hem of the monarch's garment. *Bai'a* has thus lost its earlier meaning, though it still contains the idea of promising obedience by a compact: the essential idea of joining hands has been lost, the humble posture of the subject being a necessary concession to court etiquette and the dignity of the sovereign. So general has this form of *bai'a* become that it must be regarded as valid.

As has been explained, the Caliph is the representative of the lawgiver, and acts for him in protecting religion and governing the world. The lawgiver's religious function is to compel men to observe their religious obligations, and it is his duty to secure the temporal prosperity of his subjects in his character of temporal ruler. The religious power of the Caliph is exercised through peculiarly Muslim offices which are subordinate to him. These are connected with public prayer, religious decisions, civil justice, the Jihād, or

[1] Cf. the similar act when giving a pledge in Job xvii. 3, mī hū l^{e}yādhī yittaqēa', and Prov. xvii. 18, xxii. 26.

war against unbelievers,[1] and the police—all of which are subordinate to the great imamate, which is the caliphate. The most exalted office of all is the Imamate in prayer. It is higher than the *mulk* or sovereign power in its essential nature, for the prophet's appointment of Abū Bakr to represent him in prayer was taken by the Companions to carry with it the appointment to temporal supremacy over the Muslim people. Unless the latter were dependent on the former such an assumption would have been groundless.

The government of the great mosques pertains to the Caliph, though he may refer it to the sulṭān, vizier, or qāḍi; so also the right of presiding at the five daily prayers, the Friday prayer, and those of the two great feasts and on eclipses and prayers for rain. The first four Caliphs and the Umayyads jealously guarded their privileges of presiding at public prayer, but when the caliphate became absorbed in sovereignty, and the rulers would not recognize other men as their equals in matters religious or temporal, they allowed others to replace them in presiding over public prayers.

The Caliph should appoint to the office of *mufti* the most worthy scholar and legist, and himself exercise a proper control over unworthy aspirants to that office. The Qāḍi's appointment is likewise subject to the caliphate. His office is to apply the decisions and principles of the sacred book and the *sunna* to the settlement of all disputes and actions between litigants. Originally this office was filled by the Caliph himself. 'Umar first delegated it to another. The functions of the qāḍi have been enlarged so as to include the administration of the affairs of the insane, orphans, bankrupts,

[1] 'The Mohammadan Common Law makes the fighting only a positive injunction where there is a *general summons* (that is, where the infidels invade a Mussulman territory, and the *Imām* for the time being issues a general proclamation, requiring all persons to stand forth to fight), for in this case war becomes a positive injunction with respect to the whole of the inhabitants.'—*The Hedaya or Guide; or, A Commentary on the Mussulman Laws*, translated by Charles Hamilton, London, 1791, vol. ii, Book IX, p. 141.

the testamentary dispositions of Muslims, pious benefactions, and so on. Formerly the qāḍi was charged with the righting of wrongs—a function which requires the strong hand of the magistrate to enforce its decrees. Up to Al Muhtadī the Caliphs exercised this function themselves, though sometimes they delegated it to their qāḍis. Sometimes too the qāḍis were made leaders of bands to carry the jihād into enemy territory.

The office of chief of police is a religious function based on the religious law.[1] His powers were more extensive than those of the qāḍi, for he had power to act to prevent crime and oppression. Later on the functions of these two offices were absorbed by the sulṭān whether they were confided to him by the Caliph or not. The duties of the police are of two kinds: first, to establish the guilt of suspected criminals, and to apply the legal penalties—mutilation or the *lex talionis* (sometimes the holder of this office is called *walī*), and secondly those duties which pertain to the qāḍi in relation to the punishment of evil-doers.

The office of *ḥisba* or local police carries with it a far-ranging commission. He may act in the public interest in putting down public abuses and offences against public safety or morals.

The office of inspector of coinage (*sikka*) is also religious, and is dependent on the caliphate. Certain offices have been suppressed or have fallen into desuetude, or have been absorbed into the temporal administration (*ṣārat sulṭāniyyatan*). Of the latter we may mention the government of the provinces, the vizirate, the supreme command of the army, and the collection and administration of the public revenues. Jihād has practically ceased except in a few countries; where

[1] This passage from one of the great classic writers of Islām shows how meaningless such phrases as 'the spiritual prerogatives', or 'the purely religious attributes', sound in Muslim ears. If the Chief Commissioner of Police is a religious (dīnī) office, what are 'purely religious functions', and by what word do politicians propose to translate 'spiritual' in connexion with the Caliph's jurisdiction?

it survives it is for the most part dependent on the sultanate. Another office which has disappeared is the registry of sharīfs, set up to establish the veracity or otherwise of those who claim to be descended from the prophet.

The title Commander of the Faithful (*amīr ul mu'minīn*) pertains to the caliphate. It dates from the time of the first Caliphs. When Abū Bakr was proclaimed Caliph the Companions and the rest of the Muslims hailed him as Caliph of the messenger of God. 'Umar in his turn was called 'the Caliph of the Caliph of the messenger of God'. Obviously there was no end to such a title if it was to be indefinitely extended thus to each succeeding Caliph, and so it was decided to replace it by another title. The title *amīr ul mu'minīn* was adapted from one used of the army leaders. In the Jāhiliyya the prophet was called Amīr of Mecca and Amīr of the Ḥijāz, so that when one of the Companions hailed 'Umar as *amīr ul mu'minīn* the title was generally approved and adopted. Since then the title has been inherited by succeeding Caliphs. It is not without significance that leaders of rebellion against existing authority such as the Shī'as and Abbasids at first adopted the title Imām, and after they were secure in the government claimed the title 'Commander of the Faithful'.

The title properly was a sign that its possessors reigned over the Ḥijāz, Syria, and 'Irāq, the native land of the Arabs; and though each Abbasid Caliph had a distinct name they all bore the title *amīr ul mu'minīn*. So also did the Fāṭimids of Africa and Egypt. The Umayyads of Spain followed their ancestors in not adopting titles like the Abbasids. They did not assume the title Commander of the Faithful because they could not hope to obtain possession of the caliphate, and because they did not hold the Ḥijāz, the cradle of Islam. But in the beginning of the fourth century when 'Abdu-l-Raḥmān came to the throne he took the title Al Nāṣir li Dīn Allah with the honorific *amīr ul mu'minīn*, being moved to do this by reports of the humiliations to which the Caliphs of the East were subjected. Cut off from all communication with the outside world, they were insulted and even blinded and murdered. His example was followed by his successors until ruin overtook the Arab caliphate. The Caliphs in Cairo and Morocco and the petty kings of Spain all suffered dishonour and contempt from their subjects, and with the degradation of the caliphate went the essential unity of Islam.

Our next extract is from the 'History of the Caliphs', written by Jalālu-l-Dīn Al Suyūṭī (849–911).[1] It is interesting to observe that he refuses even to mention the descendants of 'Ubaid Allah al Mahdī, who assumed the title of Caliph in 296, on the ground that the assumption of the title was illegal for many reasons, of which he thinks it sufficient to mention that he was not of the tribe of the Quraish. Moreover, Al Suyūṭī devotes some pages to discussing the question as to whether the caliphate as an office ever existed in the mind of the prophet at all.

The two shaikhs, he says, have recorded regarding 'Umar that he said when he was stabbed, 'Were I to name a successor then verily he named a successor who was greater than I (i.e. Abū Bakr). And were I to leave you without one, then verily he also hath left you so who was greater than I.'

The authority of Hudhail ibn Shurahbil is quoted to refute the claim of the Alids that Muhammad bequeathed the caliphate to 'Alī. But the objection is raised, 'Why then was not 'Alī the immediate successor of Muhammad rather than Abū Bakr?'

Writing of the fall of the caliphate he says: 'Things came to such a pass that nothing remained of the caliphate in the provinces but the name, after it had been that in the time of the children of 'Abdu-l-Malik b. Marwān the Khuṭba was read in the name of the Caliphs in all the regions of the earth, the east and the west, the right hand and the left, wherever the true believer had been victorious, and none in any one of the provinces was appointed to hold a single office

[1] Tr. by Major H. S. Jarrett, Calcutta, 1881, pp. 2 ff. (*Bibliotheca Indica*, xii, Series III).

except by order of the Caliph. Regarding the immoderate lengths to which things went, verily in the fifth century in Spain alone there were six persons who assumed the title Caliph.'

Al Suyūṭī's account[1] of the temporary restitution of the caliphate in Cairo after the death of Musta'ṣim at the hands of Hulāgū illustrates the threefold qualification required of an aspirant to the caliphate, namely, descent from the Quraish, public election and homage, and temporal power. 'He rode through Cairo, and subsequently certified his family descent through the chief Kadi Tāju-l-Dīn b. Bint Al 'Azz, and he was then acknowledged Caliph. The first who swore allegiance to him was the sulṭān, next the chief Kadi Tāju-l-Dīn . . . and lastly the nobles according to their degree. This occurred on the 13th Rajab (12 May, 1261). His name was impressed on the coinage and read in the Khuṭba, and he received the surname of his brother, and the people rejoiced. He rode in procession on the Friday, bearing the black mantle, to the mosque in the citadel. He then mounted the pulpit and preached a discourse in which he extolled the nobility of the house of 'Abbās, blessed the Caliph and the Muslims, and prayed before the people. Next he proceeded to the ceremony of the bestowal on the sulṭān of the robe of honour usually granted by the Caliph and the diploma of investiture. A pavilion was erected without the walls of Cairo, and the Caliph and the sulṭān rode to the pavilion on Monday 4th Sha'bān, and there were present the nobles, kadis, and prime minister. The Caliph with his own hand invested the sulṭān with the dress of honour. . . .'

Lastly, we may cite the views of a learned and distinguished Indian writer of to-day on this question:[2] 'Until the rise of the house of 'Abbās there was little or no difference between the assertors of the right of the Ahlu-l-Bait to the pontificate and the upholders of the right of the people to elect their own

[1] *Op. cit.*, p. 563.

[2] *The Spirit of Islam*, by Ameer Ali, Syed, Calcutta, 1902, pp. 288 ff.

spiritual and temporal chiefs. . . . The Church and State were linked together: the Caliph was the Imām—temporal chief as well as spiritual head. The doctors of law and religion were his servants. He presided at the convocations, and guided their decisions. Hence the solidarity of the Sunni church. . . . The question of the Imamate, or the spiritual headship of the Mussalman commonwealth, is henceforth the chief battle-ground of the two sects. The Shī'as hold that the spiritual heritage bequeathed by Muhammad devolved on 'Alī and his descendants. They naturally repudiate the authority of the *Jamaat* (the people) to elect a spiritual head who should supersede the rightful claims of the Prophet's family. . . .

According to the Sunnīs the Imamate is not restricted to the family of Muhammad. But no one can be elected to the office unless he is a Quraishite.'

In a note the author writes: 'There is a great difference of opinion, however, on this point. Ibn Khaldūn, being a Yemenite himself, maintained that it was not necessary for the Imām to be a Quraishite; and many Sunnī doctors have held the same view. The Sultans of Turkey have since the time of Salīm I, the father of Sulaimān the Magnificent, assumed the title of Caliph. They base their title upon a renunciation of the Caliphate and Imamate in favour of Salīm by the last Abbasid Caliph of Egypt.'

They also hold that the Imamate is indivisible, and that it is not lawful to have two Imāms at one and the same time. As Christianity could yield obedience to but one Pope, so the Muslim world could yield obedience to but one lawful Caliph. . . . As formerly, the Ummayads, the Abbasids, and the Fatimids reigned contemporaneously at Grenada, Bagdad, and Cairo; so at the present day the sovereigns of the house of Kajar and Osman possess the dignity of Caliph at Teheran and Constantinople, and the rulers of Morocco in West Africa. It must be said, however, that the Sultan of Turkey, the custodian of the two holy cities[1] and the holder

[1] The Sultan is no longer the *de facto* Guardian of the Holy Places

of the insignia of the Caliphate—the banner, the sword, and the mantle of the Prophet—has the best claim to the dignity.'

APPENDIX B

A TRANSLATION OF THE KITĀBU-L-QADAR FROM THE ṢAḤĪḤ OF AL-BUKHĀRĪ

THE following translation of the *Kitābu-l-Qadar* will show the general character of the hadith literature, and illustrate the various matters already discussed in this volume. By the kind permission of the Royal Asiatic Society it is reproduced (with the omission of the critical and historical notes that accompanied it) from my article 'Free Will and Predestination in Islam' in the *Journal of the Royal Asiatic Society* for January, 1924, pp. 42–63.

THE BOOK OF PREDESTINATION [1]

1. Bāb concerning Predestination.

(*a*) Abu'l Walīd Hishām ibn 'Abd il Mālik informed us (saying): Shu'ba informed us (saying): Sulaimān al Ā'mash told me as follows: I heard Zaid ibn Wahb on the authority of 'Abd Ullah [2] say: The Apostle of God (may God bless and

for H.M. King Ḥusain, the Amīr of Mecca, recovered this office when the Turks were driven from the Ḥaramain. He is a Sharīf of the Hashimite line.

[1] Kitābu'l Qadar 82. *Le recueil des Traditions Mahométanes*, par Abou Abdallah Mohammed ibn Ismaïl el Bokhâri, publié par M. Ludolf Krehl, continué par Th. W. Juynboll, Leyden, 1908, vol. iv, p. 251.

[2] i.e. Ibn Mas'ūd. The *isnād* will be omitted in future, only the name of the original guarantor being given.

preserve him,[1] for he is the Veracious and the Verified) told me as follows: Verily (each) one of you is assembled in his mother's womb forty days; then he becomes a clot for a similar period, and then a lump of flesh for the same period. An angel is sent to him and given four commands with reference to his sustenance, the duration of his life, and he is to be wretched or happy. By Allah! each one[2] of you may do the works of the people of hell so that between him and it there lieth but a fathom or a cubit, and that which has been written shall overcome him, and he will do the works of the people of paradise and shall enter therein. And verily a man may do the works of the people of paradise so that between him and it there lieth but a fathom or a cubit, and that which has been written shall overcome him, and he will do the works of the people of hell and shall enter therein. (Variant: Adam [i.e. Ibn Abi Iyyās] said: 'except a cubit.')

(*b*) Anas ibn Mālik. The prophet said: God commands an angel concerning the womb. The angel says: Lo, Lord, a drop! a clot! an embryo! And when God wills to decree its creation the angel says: Is it to be male or female, wretched or happy, and what is to be its sustenance and duration of life, O Lord? In the mother's womb the answer is written.

2. Bāb. The pen is dry (that wrote) according to the (fore)-knowledge of God, and the saying 'According to (fore)-knowledge God leads him astray' (Sur. xlv, v. 22). And Abū Huraira said: 'The Prophet said to me, "The pen is dry (that wrote) of what will befall thee."' Ibn 'Abbās said: With regard to the words *lahā sābiqūna* (Sur. xxiii, v. 63) the meaning is that those who hasten after good deeds happiness has hastened unto them.

(*a*) 'Imrān ibn Ḥuṣain. A man said: 'O Apostle of God, are those (destined) to paradise known from those (destined) to hell?' 'Yes,' replied he. The man answered: 'Then of what use are deeds of any kind?' He answered: 'Every one

[1] The customary blessing on Muhammad will be omitted throughout the book.

[2] Textual variant, or 'a man' of you.

does that for which he was created or that which has been made easy for him.'

3. Bāb. 'God knoweth better what they would have done.'

(*a*) Ibn 'Abbās said: The Prophet was asked about the children of idolators (*mushrikīn*). He replied: 'God knoweth better what they would have done.'

(*b*) Abū Huraira: The Apostle of God was asked about the offspring of idolators. He replied: 'God knoweth better what they would have done.'

(*c*) Abū Huraira. The Apostle of God said: 'None is born but in the religion of Islam. It is his parents who make him a Jew or a Christian just as you breed cattle. You do not find maimed cattle unless you yourselves first maim them.' They said: 'O Apostle of God, have you considered the case of him who dies as a little child?' He answered: 'God knows better what they would have done.'

4. Bāb. 'The command of God is destiny predestined' (Sur. xxxiii, v. 38).

(*a*) Abū Huraira. The Apostle of God said: 'A woman shall not ask that her sister be divorced so that she may enjoy her share of conjugal rights. Let her marry, for verily she shall have what has been decreed for her.'

(*b*) Usāma. I was in the company of the prophet when the messenger of one of his daughters came—Sa'd and Ubay ibn Ka'b and Mu'adh were with him at the time—to report that her son was at the point of death. He sent word to her: 'To God belongeth what He taketh and to God belongeth what He giveth. Every one (departeth) at the appointed time. Let her therefore be patient under bereavement and earn the reward of patience.'

(*c*) Sa'īdu-l Khudrī. The Prophet said: Every living soul whose coming forth into the world has been written by God must come into being.

(*d*) Ḥudhaifa. The prophet preached us a sermon in which he spoke of everything that will happen until the hour of the resurrection. He that knoweth it knoweth it; and he that is ignorant of it is ignorant thereof. If I see a thing which I have forgotten I shall recognize it just as a man knows the face of an absent acquaintance and recognizes him when he sees him.

(*e*) 'Ali. We were sitting with the prophet who had a stick with which he was writing on the ground. He said: 'There is not one of you whose resting place in hell or paradise has not been written.' Whereupon one of the people said: 'Then may we not (abandoning effort) trust in (our destiny), O Apostle of God?' He replied: 'No! Do (good) works for everything has been made easy.'[1] Then he read (Sur. xcii, v. 5): 'He that giveth to the needy and feareth,' &c.

5. Bāb. 'Works (are to be judged) by their results.'

(*a*) Abū Huraira said: We were present with the Apostle of God at Khaibar when he said of one of those who were with him and professed Islam: 'This fellow is one of the people of hell.' When battle was joined the man fought with the utmost bravery, insomuch that he was covered with wounds and disabled. One of the Companions of the prophet came up and said: 'O Apostle of God, do you see that the man you said was one of the people of hell has fought with the utmost bravery in the way of God and is covered with wounds.' The Prophet replied: 'Nevertheless, he is one of the people of hell.' And while some of the Muslims were on the point of doubting, lo the man, in anguish from his wounds, put forth his hand to his quiver, plucked out an arrow, and pierced his throat therewith. Some of the Muslims then ran to the Apostle of God and said: 'O Apostle of God, God has confirmed thy saying. So-and-so has pierced his throat and killed himself.' The Apostle of God said: 'O Bilāl, rise and proclaim: Only believers shall enter paradise. Verily God strengtheneth this religion with an impious man.'

(*b*) Sahl. The prophet looked at a man who did most service to the Muslims on a raid he made in company with the prophet, and said: 'He who would see one of the people of hell let him look at this fellow.' So one of the people followed him—now he was the most violent of men in contending with the idolators—until he was wounded, when he

[1] Or prepared. See *Al-Nihāya in loc.*

proceeded to hasten his death by putting his sword point to his breast so that it came out between his shoulders. The man quickly went to the prophet and said: 'I bear witness that thou art the Apostle of God!' He said: 'But why?' The man replied: 'Thou saidst of So-and-so, "He who would see one of the people of hell let him look at this fellow." Now he was one who did the Muslims most service, and thou knewest that he would not die thus. And when he was wounded he hastened his death by suicide.' Thereupon the prophet said: 'Verily the slave may do the works of the people of hell when he is really one of the people of paradise. And he may do the works of the people of paradise when he is really one of the people of hell. Actions are to be judged by their results.'

6. Bāb. A vow delivers a slave to fate.

(*a*) Ibn 'Umar. The prophet forbade vows, saying: 'Verily they cannot frustrate anything though something is extracted from the avaricious thereby.'

(*b*) Abū Huraira. A vow brings nothing to a son of man that has not been decreed for him. Nevertheless, a vow does precipitate a man towards (his) destiny, and it has been decreed that something shall be extracted from the avaricious thereby.

7. Bāb. There is no power and no might save in God.

(*a*) Abū Mūsā. We were raiding with the Apostle of God, and whenever we climbed or ascended a height or went down into a valley we lifted up our voices and shouted, 'Allah Akbar!' The Apostle of God approached us and said: 'Restrain yourselves, O men. For ye do not call to one who is deaf or absent, but ye call to one who hears and sees.' Then he said: 'O 'Abd Allah ibn Qais, I will teach thee a saying which is one of the treasures of paradise, "There is no power and no might save in God."'

8. Bāb. The Protected is he whom God protects ('aṣama) (in Sur. xi, v. 45, the word 'āṣima is the equivalent of māni'a). Mujāhid said: saddan (in Sur. xxxvi, v. 8, 'we have placed before and behind them an obstacle' means) a barrier against

the truth. They repeatedly fall into error. The word dassāhā (Sur. xci, v. 10, in 'Miserable is he who has corrupted it' [i.e. the soul] means) aghwāhā misled.

(*a*) Sa'īdu-l Khudrī. Every one who is appointed Caliph has two kinds of intimates: one advises him to do good and incites him thereto; the other suggests and incites to evil. The protected is he whom God protects.

9. Bāb. It is a necessary lot of (the people) of a city which we have destroyed that they shall not return (Sur. xxi, v. 95). None of thy people will believe save those who have already believed (Sur. xi, v. 38). 'And they will beget only impious unbelievers' (Sur. lxxi, v. 28).

(*a*) Ibn 'Abbās. The word ḥirm in Abyssinian means wajaba.

(*b*) Ibn 'Abbās. Nothing seems to me more insane than Abū Huraira's report that the Prophet said: 'God has written every man's portion in adultery. It must certainly befall. Now it is adultery of the eye to gaze; it is adultery of the tongue to utter (the thought thus engendered); the appetite longs and desires and the body consents or denies.' (Here follows the isnadic authority for the hadith of Abū Huraira to which Ibn 'Abbās takes exception.)

10. Bāb. We have made the vision that we showed thee a cause of dissension for men (Sur. xvii, v. 62).

(*a*) Ibn 'Abbās. This is the vision of the eye which the Apostle of God was shown when he was conducted on the night journey to the temple of Jerusalem. He said: 'The tree which is cursed in the Quran' is the tree of Al Zaqqūm.

11. Bāb. Adam and Moses argued before God (to Him belong might and majesty).

(*a*) Abū Huraira. The Prophet said: 'Adam and Moses were arguing, and Moses said: "O Adam, thou art our father. Thou hast brought loss upon us and caused us to be excluded from paradise." He replied: "O Moses, God chose thee by His word and wrote for thee with His hand. Do you blame me for a matter which God decreed concerning me forty years before He created me?" And Adam confuted Moses three times.' (The same tradition is reported with a change of two names in the intermediaries between Abū Huraira and the compiler.)

12. Bāb. None can withhold what God giveth.

(*a*) Warrād, the client of Al Mughīra ibn Shu'ba. Mu'āwīya wrote to Al Mughīra as follows: 'Write for me an account of what you heard the prophet say at the end of the prescribed prayer.' Al Mughīra then dictated to me: 'I heard the prophet say at the end of the prescribed prayer, "There is no God save God alone; he is without associate. O God, there is none that withholdest what Thou givest and none that giveth what Thou withholdest, and good fortune will not profit the fortunate in place of Thee."' Ibn Juraij said 'Abda told him that Warrād told him of this. 'Then', said he, 'I afterwards went on a mission to Mu'āwīya and heard him laying commands on men in accordance with these words.'

13. Bāb. He that taketh refuge in God from the misery that overtaketh him and from the evil of fate. And God's Word: 'Say: I take refuge in the Lord of the Dawn from the evil He hath created' (Sur. 113).

(*a*) Abū Huraira. The prophet said: 'Take refuge in God from grievous adversity, from misery that overtaketh, from evil fate, and from the reviling of enemies.'

14. Bāb. (God) intervenes between a man and his heart (Sur. viii, v. 24).

(*a*) 'Abd Ullah. The prophet used often to take an oath 'No, by the Reverser of hearts!'

(*b*) Ibn 'Umar. The prophet said to Ibn Ṣayyād: 'I have a riddle to ask of thee.' He replied: 'Smoke.' The prophet said: 'Go away, for thou shalt not exceed thy measure (*qadr*).' 'Umar said: 'Give me permission to strike off his head!' The prophet replied: 'Let him alone. If it is he (the Dajjāl) you cannot do it, and if it is not he then you will gain nothing by killing him.'

15. Bāb. Say 'Nought will befall us save what God has written for us' ('written' here means) 'decreed' (Sur. ix, v. 51). Mujāhid said: (In Sur. xxxvii, v. 162, the word)

bifātinīn means bimuḍillīn (ye are not able to) seduce means 'lead astray', save those of whom God has written that they shall burn in Gehenna. 'He decreeth and guideth' (Sur. lxxxvii, v. 3) means 'He decreeth misery and happiness and He guideth the sheep to their pastures'.

(*a*) 'Āisha said that she asked the Apostle of God about the plague. He replied: 'It is a punishment which God sends against whom He wills. And God makes it a mercy to believers. There is not a servant in a plague-stricken country who remains therein without removing thence in patient belief, knowing that nought will befall him save what God has written for him, but receives the reward of a martyr.'

16. Bāb. We should not be guided aright were it not that God guideth us (Sur. vii, v. 41). Had God guided me, verily I had been of the godly (Sur. xxxix, v. 58).

(*a*) Al Barā ibn 'Āzib. I saw the prophet on the 'day of the Trench' helping us to remove the earth, saying the while:

'If God were not our Guide, then we should stray
From His straight paths and should not fast nor pray.
Then keep us strong and calm in danger's hour;
Stablish our feet by Thy almighty power.
The idolators have wrong'd us, we sought peace,
But they, rebelling, fight and will not cease.'

BIBLIOGRAPHY OF WORKS CITED

Ameer Ali. *The Spirit of Islam*, Calcutta, 1902.

Arnold, Sir T. W. *The Preaching of Islam*, London, 1913.

Asin et Palacios, Michael. *Logia et Agrapha domini Jesu apud Moslemicos scriptores, asceticos praesertim, usitata . . . Patrologia Orientalis*, Tome xiii, Fasc. 3, Paris (n. d.).

—— *La Escatologia Musulmana en la Divina Comedia*, Madrid, 1919.

Abū Dāūd. *Sunan*, Cairo, 1280.

Ibnu-l-Athīr. *Nihāya*, Cairo, 1311. 2 vols.

'Alā-al-Dīn Al Muttaqī. *Kanzu-l-'Ummāl*, Haidarabad, 1894.

Al Bukhārī. *Le Recueil des traditions mahométanes*, ed. L. Krehl and T. Juynboll, Leyden, 1908.

Burton, Sir R. F. *Personal Narrative of a Pilgrimage to Al-Madinah and Meccah.* 2 vols., London, 1915–19.

Bevan, E. *Jerusalem under the High Priests*, Cambridge, 1910.

Caetani, Prince L. *Annali dell' Islam*, Milan, 1905.

Cheragh Ali. *A Critical Exposition of the Popular Jihad*, Calcutta, 1888.

—— *The Proposed Political . . . Reforms in the Ottoman Empire and other Muhammadan States.*

Doughty, G. *Arabia Deserta*, Cambridge, 1923.

Driver, S. R. *A Critical . . . Commentary on Deuteronomy*, Edinburgh, 1902.

Goldziher, I. *Muhammadanische Studien*, Halle, 1889.

—— *Vorlesungen über den Islam*, Heidelberg, 1910.

Guillaume, A. Predestination and Free Will in Islam, *JRAS*, Jan., 1924.

Hamilton, Charles. *The Hedaya, or A Commentary on the Mussulman Laws*, London, 1791.

Houdas, O. et Marcais, W. *Les Traditions islamiques traduites par . . .* 4 vols. Paris, 1903–14.

Ibn Hanbal. *Musnad*, Cairo, 1890.

Jarrett, H. S. *History of the Caliphs* (Bibliotheca Indica, xii, Series III), Calcutta, 1881.

JASB. *Journal of the Asiatic Society of Bengal.*
JAOS. *Journal of the American Oriental Society.*
JA. *Journal Asiatique.*
JRAS. *Journal of the Royal Asiatic Society.*
Ibn Khaldun *Muqaddima*, Beyrout.
Al Kindī. *Risāla*, London, 1880.
Lane, E. W. *The Manners and Customs of the Modern Egyptians*, London, 1917.
—— *Arabian Society in the Middle Ages*, London, 1883.
Lammens, H. *Études sur le règne du calife Omayade Moawia Ier*, Beyrout, 1906.
Al Mas'ūdī. *Les Prairies d'Or, texte et traduction*, par S. Barbier de Meynard. 9 vols. Paris, 1861–77.
Macdonald, D. B. *Development of Muslim Theology, Jurisprudence, and Constitutional Theory*, London, 1903.
Ibn Māja. *Sunan*, Delhi, 1282.
Margoliouth, D. S. *The Early Development of Muhammadanism*, London, 1914.
—— *Muhammad and the Rise of Islam*, London, 1905.
Muir, Sir W. *Life of Muhammad*, revised by T. H. Weir, Edinburgh, 1912.
—— *Annals of the Early Caliphate*, London, 1883.
Nicholson, R. A. *A Literary History of the Arabs*, London, 1907.
Nöldeke, T.-Schwally. *Geschichte des Qorans*, Leipzig, 1919.
Ibn Qutaiba. *Mukhtalifu-l-hadith*, Cairo, 1317.
Al Qasṭallānī. *Irshādu-l-Sārī*, Bulaq, 1305. 10 vols.
Abu Qurra. *Mujādala*, MS. arabe, No. 70, Bibliothèque Nationale.
Rodwell, M. *The Quran*, London, 1861.
Al Suyūṭī. *Ta'rīkhu-l-Khulafā*, Cairo, 1305.
Sprenger, A. *Das Leben und die Lehre des Mohammad.* 3 vols. Berlin, 1861–5.
—— *Dictionary of Technical Terms*, Calcutta, 1862.
Ibn Ṭabāṭaba. *Al Fakhrī*, Cairo, 1280.
Taylor, C. W. *Sayings of the Jewish Fathers*, Cambridge, 1897.
Talmud Babli. Vilna.
Wüstenfeld. *Wafayātu-l-A'yān of Ibn Khallikān.*
Wāliu-l-Dīn Abū 'Abd Allah. *Mishkātu-l-Maṣābīḥ*, Bombay, 1880.
Zwemer, S. M. *The Influence of Animism on Islam*, London, 1920.
ZDMG. *Zeitschrift der deutschen morgenländischen Gesellschaft.*

A GLOSSARY OF THE MORE COMMON TECHNICAL TERMS USED IN THE HADITH LITERATURE

'azīz. *Precious.* An authentic tradition coming from two Companions.

ḍa'īf. Not fulfilling the required conditions.

fard. See *gharīb.*

gharīb. Authentic, but resting on the authority of only one Companion.

ḥasan. Of *fair* authority; with a slight fault.

ijmālī. Referring to many things.

maḥfūẓ. One of two suspicious traditions which has a slight advantage over its rival.

manqūl. Handed down by tradition.

mansūkh. Abrogated.

maqbūl. *Received* generally; fulfilling all conditions.

maqlūb. Known to have come from a person other than the *soi-disant* reporter.

maqṭū'. An *isnād* which is interrupted or *cut off.*

mardūd. A tradition from a doubtful source which contradicts a tradition of good standing.

marfū'. Record of a word or deed of the prophet reported by the Companion who heard or saw it.

ma'rūf. Weak, yet *known* because it is confirmed by another.

mashhūr. A tradition vouched for by more than two Companions.

mauḍū'. False.

mauqūf. An *isnād* going back to the Companions, but *stopping* short of the prophet.

mu'allal. An *isnād* or text with a hidden fault.

mu'allaq. *Suspended,* i. e. without the name of the Companion.

mubham. Coming from one of whom one knows nothing but the name.

mu'ḍal. An *isnād* from which a name has disappeared.

mudallas. A tradition falsely ascribed to an early authority.

mudraj. A gloss or observation inserted by one of the first reporters of the tradition.

muḍṭarab. A tradition in which a word has become *misplaced,* added, or suppressed, or suffered any kind of derangement.

mukhtalif. Two traditions which are in apparent contradiction, but which can be reconciled.

munkar. A tradition of weak authority contradicted by a weaker one.

munqaṭaʿ. An *isnād* from which a name has disappeared.

mursal. A text without *isnād*, or one with an incomplete *isnād*, or without the name of the Follower.

muṣaḥḥaf. An *isnād* in which a name is badly written; or, a text in which a word is badly written.

musalsal. With a *chain* of authorities reaching back to the prophet.

mushkal. Of doubtful authority.

musnad. A tradition whose *isnād* goes back to the prophet. A collection of such *supported* traditions.

mustafīḍ. See *mashhūr*.

mutābiʿ. A tradition similar in import to another one going back to the same authority.

mutawātir. Reported by numerous authorities.

mutqin. Accurate reporter.

muttafaq ʿalaihi. Received by Bukhārī and Muslim.

muttaṣal. A tradition with an uninterrupted *isnād*.

nāsikh. Abrogating.

rāwi. One who reports a tradition.

ṣaḥīḥ. Genuine; fulfilling all conditions.

shādhdh. Exceptional. A tradition of good authority yet in conflict with another similarly attested.

shāhid. A tradition from a Companion *bearing witness to* or confirming one from another Companion.

ṭarīq. The *route*, or reporters, by which the tradition has come.

thiqa. Trustworthy reporter.

ADDENDA

p. 23. The earliest extant *musnad* is that of Abū Dāūd Sulaimān al-Ṭayālisī (133–203). His authorities were Al-Thaurī, Shuʿba, Hishām and others. It is recorded by one of his contemporaries, Muhammad b. Minhāl al-Ḍarīr, that he proved him guilty of falsely propagating traditions in the name of Ibn ʿAun. Al-Ṭayālisī's most celebrated pupil was Aḥmad b. Ḥanbal. This note is based on al-Samʿāni, *Kitābu-l-Ansāb*, (Gibb facsimile) 1913, p. 374 *ult.*, and I owe the reference to Dr. Nicholson.

p. 68, l. 17. 'spread their wings over' *taḍaʿu ajniḥatahā li-ṭālibi-l-ʿilm*, see *Nihāya*, vol. I, p. 182, under *janaḥ*. I prefer this, the last of many explanations offered by the commentators. An abridged form of this hadith will be found on p. 4 of Derenbourg's edition of *Al-Fakhrī*. M. Amar (*Histoire des dynasties musulmanes*, Paris, 1910, p. 3) renders: 'the angels lower their wings to carry the seeker after knowledge'; this, I suppose, is implied by Ibnu-l-Athir when he explains: 'wiṭā'an lahu idhā mashā.'

INDEX